C000133361

SMALL TALK

# Asia

# 10
ESSENTIAL
LANGUAGES FOR
CITY BREAKS &
BUSINESS TRAVEL

**Small Talk Asia**
1st edition – March 2008

**Published by**
Lonely Planet Publications Pty Ltd ABN 36 005 607 983
90 Maribyrnong St, Footscray, Victoria 3011, Australia

**Lonely Planet Offices**
**Australia** Locked Bag 1, Footscray, Victoria 3011
**USA** 150 Linden St, Oakland CA 94607
**UK** 2nd Floor, 186 City Road, London, EC1V 2NT

**Commissioning Editor** Karin Vidstrup Monk **Series Designer** Yukiyoshi Kamimura **Editor** Branislava Vladisavljevic **Layout Designer** Wibowo Rusli **Cartographer** Wayne Murphy **Special Sections Contributor** Jodie Martire

**Authors** Yoshi Abe, Chiu-yee Cheung, Leviseda Douglas, Bruce Evans, Anthony Garnaut, Ben Handicott, Jonathan Hilts-Park, San San Hnin Tun, Momoko Honda, Yuanfang Ji, Minkyoung Kim, Tao Li, Jason Roberts, Natrudy Saykao, Bill Tuffin, Laszlo Wagner

**Cover** Giggling girls, Dominic Arizona Bonuccelli/Lonely Planet Images; Architecture, Krzysztof Dydyński/Lonely Planet Images

ISBN 978 1 74179 142 6

# Korean 63

# Lao 73

# Mandarin 83

# Thai 93

# Vietnamese 103

# 24 hours in the city 113

# Index 124

4

# Asia – at a glance

Going away for the day, the weekend or the classic short break? *Small Talk Asia* gives you the essential language you need to live it up in Asia. Get hot sightseeing tips in our '24 hours in the city' feature and talk your way to the best soup stalls in Phnom Penh, the A-list shopping centres in Seoul or a Yanjing beer in Beijing. Dip into our 'Festivals' feature, get your party shoes on and join in this exciting region's sizzling cultural life.

A bit about the languages ... Only Vietnamese and Indonesian – both written in Roman script – might look familiar to you. For the rest, get ready for a reading adventure. Korean, in addition to being linked to Japanese, is part of the Ural-Altaic family (along with Turkish and Mongolian). Japanese has no clear links to any other languages, but it's written in a combination of Chinese kanji characters and two indigenous scripts. Thai, Lao, Burmese and Khmer can all be traced to the Sanskrit and Pali languages of India. Mandarin is known as *Putonghua* (meaning 'the common dialect') in its homeland, but to make yourself understood in Hong Kong, Cantonese will be your first choice. Whichever language – this is one region sure to set the senses in overdrive.

## did you know?

- Asia is the largest and most heavily populated continent on Earth. It's home to nearly 60% of the current world population – China, Indonesia and Japan all rank among the 10 most populous nations – on nearly 30% of the world's land area.
- The first use of the name 'Asia' for this region is attributed to Herodotus in about 440BC, when he used it to talk about Anatolia or Persia in the Persian Wars.
- Marco Polo, in a 1292 account of his travels to Asia, can be credited with igniting Europe's feverish hunt for a quick sea passage to the aromatic Spice Islands. Spices, used in European burial rituals and as both flavouring and preservative for food, were once far more precious than gold.

## abbreviations

The abbreviations mark the subject (Burmese) or the speaker (Thai):

| | | | |
|---|---|---|---|
| f | feminine | m | masculine |

Sea of Okhotsk

Kuril Is (Disputed)

Harbin

Changchun

Shenyang

**Beijing** ✪ **Pyongyang** NORTH KOREA

Tianjin **Seoul** ✪

SOUTH KOREA

Jinan Yellow Sea (West Sea) JAPAN

Xi'an Nanjing Shanghai Fukuoka Kyushu

Wuhan Hangzhou East China Sea

Sapporo Hokkaido

Honshu Sendai

Osaka ✪ **Tokyo** Nagoya

**Taipei** ✪

Guangzhou Shantou TAIWAN

Macau Hong Kong Kaohsiung

Hue South China Sea

**Cantonese**

CHINA

Wuzhou

Nanning ○ Guangzhou

VIETNAM Macau ○ Hong Kong

Zhanjiang

Gulf of Tonkin

South China Sea

Kota Kinabalu Philippines

Brunei ● Sabah

MALAYSIA Sarawak

Kuching Celebes Sea

Borneo Palau Micronesia

INDONESIA Moluccas

Banjarmasin Celebes Ambon Jayapura

Bandung Java Sea Banda Irian Jaya

Bali Surabaya Makassar Sea Papua New Guinea

Denpasar East Timor Solomon Sea

Kupang Arafura Sea

Timor Sea

Australia

■ ✪ Mandarin (official)

▨ Mandarin (widely understood)

■ Thai

■ Vietnamese

*Note: Language areas are approximate only.*

ASIA

# January

| | | |
|---|---|---|
| Lunar New Year | **China, South Korea, Vietnam** | Jan/Feb |
| Seijin No Hi (Coming of Age Day) | **Japan** | 8th |

# February

| | | |
|---|---|---|
| Huong Tich (Perfume Pagoda Festival) | **Vietnam** | Feb/Mar |
| Magha Puja (Buddhist celebration) | **Laos, Thailand** | Feb/Mar |
| Sapporo Yuki Matsuri (Sapporo Snow Festival) | **Japan** | |
| Shwedagon Festival (pagoda festival) | **Myanmar** | Feb/Mar |
| Yuanxiao (Lantern Festival) | **China** | Feb/Mar |

# March

| | | |
|---|---|---|
| Bun Wat Phu Champasak (Buddhist festival at Wat Phu Temple) | **Laos** | |
| Cow-Racing Festival (Khmer ethnic festival) | **Vietnam** | |
| Hanami (Cherry Blossom Viewing) | **Japan** | Mar/Apr |
| Hina Matsuri (Doll Festival) | **Japan** | 3rd |
| Muharram (Muslim New Year) | **Indonesia** | Mar/Apr |
| Nyepi (Hindu New Year) | **Indonesia** | Mar/Apr |

# April

| | | |
|---|---|---|
| Arirang (mass gymnastics & sports display) | **North Korea** | 15th |
| Chaul Chnam (Khmer New Year) | **Cambodia** | |

| Ching Ming (Remembrance of Ancestors' Day) | China | 4th or 5th |
|---|---|---|
| Elephant Race Festival | Vietnam | |
| Kanamara Matsuri (Festival of the Steel Phalus – fertility festival) | Japan | 30 Apr–1 May |
| Pii Mai (Lunar New Year) | Laos | |
| Songkran Festival (water festival) | Thailand | |
| Thingyan (Water Festival) | Myanmar | |
| Tin Hau Day (fishermen's festival) | China | |

## May

| Bun Bang Fai (Rocket Festival – rain-making festival) | Laos | 1st week |
|---|---|---|
| Bun Festival (parades, performances & climbing up bun towers) | Hong Kong | |
| Giong (festival in honour of the legendary national hero, Saint Giong) | Vietnam | May/Jun |
| Sanja Matsuri (festival of the Asakusa Shrine) | Japan | |
| Tosho-gu Shrine Festival | Japan | |
| Vishka Puja (Buddha's birth) | Cambodia, Laos, Thailand | May/Jun |

## June

| Dano Festival (processions of shamans & mask dances) | South Korea | Jun/Jul |
|---|---|---|
| Tiet Doan Ngo (Summer Solstice Festival) | Vietnam | around the 23rd |
| Tuen Ng Festival (Double Fifth – Dragon Boat Festival) | Hong Kong | |

## July

| | | |
|---|---|---|
| Gion Matsuri (thanksgiving festival) | **Japan** | 2nd |
| Khao Phansa (beginning of the three-month Buddhist Lent) | **Laos, Thailand** | |
| Qixi (Double Seventh Festival – Chinese Valentine's Day) | **China** | |
| Tet Trung Nguyen (Buddhist pagoda celebration) | **Vietnam** | |

## August

| | | |
|---|---|---|
| Awa Odori (traditional dancing festival) | **Japan** | |
| Queen's Birthday (Mother's Day) | **Thailand** | 12th |
| Tet Trung Thu (Mid-Autumn Festival) | **Vietnam** | 15th |
| Yue Laan (Hungry Ghost Festival – ancestor worship) | **China** | Aug/Sep |

## September

| | | |
|---|---|---|
| Awk Phansa (end of the three-month Buddhist Lent) | **Laos, Thailand** | Sep/Oct |
| Chongyang (Double Ninth Festival – Ying & Yang) | **China** | |
| Chuesok (Harvest Moon Festival) | **South Korea** | Sep/Oct |
| Kiep Bac Festival (commemorating national hero general Tran Quoc Tuan) | **Vietnam** | Sep/Oct |
| P'chum Ben (commemorating the spirits of the dead) | **Cambodia** | Sep/Oct |

| Thadingyut (Festival of Lights – end of Buddhist Lent) | Myanmar | Sep/Oct |
| --- | --- | --- |
| Zhongqiu (Mooncake Festival – mid-autumn festival) | China | |

## October

| Bun Nam (water festival) | Laos | late Oct |
| --- | --- | --- |
| Chulalongkorn Day (in honour of King Chulalongkorn) | Thailand | 23rd |
| Kathein (offerings to the monastic community) | Myanmar | Oct/Nov |
| Rice Harvest Festivals | Cambodia | Oct–Jan |
| Takayama Matsuri (parade of large decorated floats) | Japan | 9th–10th (also 14–15 Apr) |

## November

| Bon Om Tuk (water festival with boat races) | Cambodia | early Nov |
| --- | --- | --- |
| Loi Krathong (Festival of Lights) | Thailand | |
| Monkeys' Banquet | Thailand | Nov/Dec |
| Shichi-Go-San (festival for children aged three, five or seven) | Japan | 15th |

## December

| Chichibu Yomatsuri (night festival with floats) | Japan | |
| --- | --- | --- |
| Dongzhi (Winter Solstice Festival) | China | 23rd |
| Karen people New Year | Myanmar | Dec/Jan |
| Lebaran or Idul Fitri (end of Ramadan) | Indonesia | |

Festivals

# Asian tone languages

If you listen to people speaking certain Asian languages you might notice that some vowels are pronounced with a high or low pitch, while others swoop or glide in an almost musical manner. That's because these languages use a system of tones to make distinctions between words. Six of the ten languages in this book use tones: Burmese, Cantonese, Lao, Mandarin, Thai and Vietnamese. In our pronunciation guides for these languages, we've represented the tones with markers on the vowels. Note that in the tables below, we've used the vowel 'a' as an example only, and that the neutral (ie level or mid) tones have no markers. Don't worry if you find it tricky to use the tones – you'll generally be understood in context even if you don't always get them right.

| Burmese | | |
|---|---|---|
| high, creaky (as in 'heart') | plain high (as in 'car') | low |
| á | à | a |

| Cantonese | | | | | |
|---|---|---|---|---|---|
| high | high rising | level | low falling | low rising | low |
| à | á | a | à | á | a |

| Lao & Thai | | | | |
|---|---|---|---|---|
| mid | low | falling | high | rising |
| a | à | â | á | ă |

| Mandarin | | | | |
|---|---|---|---|---|
| high | high rising | low falling-rising | high falling | neutral |
| ā | á | ǎ | à | a |

| Vietnamese | | | | | |
|---|---|---|---|---|---|
| mid level | low falling | low rising | high broken * | high rising | low broken # |
| a | à | ả | ã | á | ạ |

\* starts high, dips slightly, then rises sharply
\# starts low, falls to a lower level, then stops

# Burmese

Myanmar's rich and thrilling culture –
dozens of languages and peoples – is a
natural drawcard.

# Pronunciation

| Vowels | | Consonants | |
|---|---|---|---|
| **Symbol** | **English sound** | **Symbol** | **English sound** |
| a | **father** | b | **bed** |
| ai | **aisle** | ch | **cheat** (aspirated) |
| aw | **saw** | d | **dog** |
| ay | **say** | dh | **that** |
| e | **bet** | g | **go** |
| i | **hit** | h | **hat** |
| oh | **note** | hl | **lot** (aspirated) |
| oo | **zoo** | hm | **man** (aspirated) |
| ow | **how** | hn | **not** (aspirated) |
| u | **put** | hng | **ring** (aspirated) |
| uh | **run** | hny | **canyon** (aspirated) |

In Burmese, there's a difference between the aspirated consonants (pronounced with a puff of air after the sound) and the unaspirated ones – you'll get the idea if you hold your hand in front of your mouth to feel your breath, and say 'pit' (where the 'p' is aspirated) and 'spit' (where it's unaspirated). The five sounds represented in our pronunciation guides with an 'h' before the consonant (hl, hm, hn, hng and hny) are pronounced with a puff of air before the consonant. The apostrophe (') stands for the sound heard between 'uh-oh'. Each syllable is separated by a dot, for example tuh-şay'·low'. For **tones**, see page 12.

| | |
|---|---|
| j | **joke** |
| k | **kit** (aspirated) |
| l | **lot** |
| m | **man** |
| n | **not** |
| ng | **ring** |
| ny | **canyon** |
| p | **pet** |
| s | **sun** |
| ş | **sun** (aspirated) |
| sh | **shot** |
| t | **top** (aspirated) |
| th | **thin** |
| w | **win** |
| y | **yes** |
| z | **zero** |

Burmese

14

# essentials

| | | |
|---|---|---|
| Yes./No. | ဟုတ်ကဲ့။/ဟင့်အင်း။ | hoh'·ké/híng·ìn |
| Hello. | မင်္ဂလာပါ။ | ming·guh·la·ba |
| Goodbye. | သွားမယ်နော်။ | thwà·me·naw |
| Please. | တဆိတ်လောက်။ | tuh·say'·low' |
| Thank you (very much). | ကျေးဇူး (အများကြီး) တင်ပါတယ်။ | chày·zù (uh·myà·jì) ting·ba·deh |
| You're welcome. | ရပါတယ်။ | yà·ba·de |
| Excuse me./Sorry. | ဆောရီးနော်။ | sàw·rì·naw |
| | | |
| Do you speak English? | အင်္ဂလိပ်လို ပြောတတ်သလား။ | ìng·guh·lay'·loh pyàw·da'·thuh·là |
| Do you understand? | နားလည်သလား။ | nà·le·dhuh·là |
| I understand. | နားလည်တယ်။ | nà·le·de |
| I don't understand. | နားမလည်ဘူး။ | nà·muh·le·bòo |

# chatting

## introductions

**Burmese**

| | | |
|---|---|---|
| Mr | ဦး | òo |
| Mrs | ဒေါ် | daw |
| Miss | မ | má |

**How are you?**
နေကောင်းလား။    nay·kòwng·là

**Fine. And you?**
ကောင်းပါတယ်။    kòwng·ba·de
ခင်များ/ရှင်ရော။    kuhng·myà/shing·yàw m/f

**What's your name?**
နာမည် ဘယ်လို ခေါ်သလဲ။    nang·me be·loh kaw·dhuh·lè

**My name is ...**
ကျွန်တော်/ကျွန်မ နာမည်က    chuh·náw/chuh·má nang·me·gá
--- ပါ။    ... ba m/f

**I'm pleased to meet you.**
တွေ့ရတာ ဝမ်းသာပါတယ်။    twáy·yá·da wùng·tha·ba·de

15

| | | |
|---|---|---|
| **Here's my ...** | ဒီမှာ ကျနော့်/ ကျမ --- ပါ။ | di·hma chuh·náw/ chuh·má ... ba **m/f** |
| **What's your ...?** | ခင်ဗျား/ရှင့် --- က ဘာလဲ။ | kuhng·myà/shíng ... gá ba·lè **m/f** |
| **email address** | အီးမေးလ် | ì·màyl |
| **phone number** | ဖုန်းနံပါတ် | pòhng·nuhng·buh' |
| **What's your occupation?** | ဘာအလုပ် လုပ်သလဲ။ | ba·uh·loh' loh'·thuh·lè |
| **I'm a/an ...** | ကျနော့်/ကျမ က --- ပါ။ | chuh·naw/chuh·má gá ... ba **m/f** |
| **businessperson** | စီးပွားရေးသမား | sì·bwà·yày dhuh·mà |
| **student** | ကျောင်းသား | chòwng·dhà **m** |
| | ကျောင်းသူ | chòwng·dhu **f** |
| **Where are you from?** | ဘယ်က လာသလဲ။ | be·gá la·dhuh·lè |
| **I'm from (England).** | (အင်္ဂလန်) ကပါ။ | (ing·guh·lang) gá·ba |
| **Are you married?** | အိမ်ထောင် ရှိသလား။ | ayng·downg shí·dhuh·là |
| **I'm ...** | ကျနော်/ကျမ က --- | chuh·naw/chuh·má gá ... **m/f** |
| **married** | အိမ်ထောင် ရှိပါတယ် | ayng·downg shí·ba·de |
| **single** | လူပျိုပါ | loo·byoh·ba **m** |
| | အပျိုပါ | uh·pyoh·ba **f** |

**How old are you?**

ခင်ဗျား/ရှင့် အသက် ဘယ်လောက်လဲ။ — kuhng·myà/shíng uh·the' be·low'·lè **m/f**

**I'm ... years old.**

ကျနော်/ကျမက --- နှစ် ရှိပြီ။ — chuh·naw/chuh·má·gá ... hni' shí·bi **m/f**

# making conversation

**What's the weather like?**

ရာသီဥတု ဘယ်လိုလဲ။ — ya·dhi·ú·dú be·loh·lè

| | | |
|---|---|---|
| **It's cold.** | အေးတယ်။ | ày·de |
| **It's (very) hot.** | (သိပ်) ပူတယ်။ | (thay') poo·de |
| **It's rainy.** | မိုးရွာနေတယ်။ | mòh·ywa·nay·de |
| **It's warm.** | နည်းနည်း ပူတယ်။ | nè·nè poo·de |

**Do you live here?**
ဒီမှာ နေသလား။ di·hma nay·dhuh·là

**What are you doing?**
အခု ဘာလုပ်နေသလဲ။ uh·gú ba·loh'·nay·dhuh·lè

## meeting up

**What time will we meet?**
ဘယ်အချိန် တွေ့ကြမလဲ။ be·uh·chayng twáy·já·muh·lè

**Where will we meet?**
ဘယ်မှာ တွေ့ကြမလဲ။ be·hma twáy·já·muh·lè

| Let's meet at ... | --- မှာ | ... hma |
|---|---|---|
| | တွေ့ကြရအောင်။ | twáy·já·yá·owng |
| (eight) o'clock | (ရှစ်)နာရီ | (shi')·na·yi |
| the entrance | အဝင်ဝ | uh·wing·wá |

**It's been great meeting you.**
တွေ့ရတာ အရမ်း twáy·yá·da uh·yàng
ဝမ်းသာတာပဲ။ wùng·tha·da·bè

## I love it here!
ဒီမှာ သိပ်ကြိုက်တာပဲ။
di·hma thay'·chai'·ta·bè

## likes & dislikes

| I thought it was ... | --- ထင်ပါတယ်။ | ... ting·ba·de |
|---|---|---|
| It's ... | ၁) --- | da ... |
| awful | အရမ်း ဆိုးတယ်။ | uh·yàng şòh·de |
| great | အရမ်း | uh·yàng |
| | ကောင်းတယ်။ | kòwng·de |
| interesting | စိတ်ဝင်စားစရာ | say'·win·zà·zuh·ya |
| | ကောင်းတယ်။ | kòwng·de |

| Do you like ...? | --- ကြိုက်သလား။ | ... chai'·thuh·là |
|---|---|---|
| I like ... | --- ကြိုက်တယ်။ | ... chai'·te |
| I don't like ... | --- မကြိုက်ဘူး။ | ... muh·chai'·pòo |
| art | အနုပညာ | uh·nú·pying·nya |
| sport | အားကစား | à·guh·zà |

17

# eating & drinking

| I'd like ..., please. | --- လိုချင်ပါတယ်။ | ... loh·jing·ba·de |
| the nonsmoking section | ဆေးလိပ်မသောက်ရတဲ့နေရာ | sày·lay' muh·thow'·yá·dé nay· |
| the smoking section | ဆေးလိပ်သောက်လို့ရတဲ့နေရာ | sày·lay' thow'·lóh·yá·dé nay· |
| a table for (four) | (၄)ယောက်စာ စားပွဲ | (làY)·yow'·sa zuh·bw |

**Do you have vegetarian food?**

သက်သတ်လွတ် စားစရာ
ရှိသလား။    the'·tha'·lu' sà·zuh·ya
shí·dhuh·là

**What would you recommend?**

ဘာမှာရင် ကောင်းမလဲ။    ba·hma·ying kòwng·muh·lè

## Would you like a drink?
တခုခု သောက်မလား။
tuh·kú·gú thow'·muh·là

| I'll have a ... | --- ယူမယ်။ | ... yoo·me |
| Cheers! | ချီးယားး။ | chì·yà |

| I'd like (the) ..., please. | --- ပေးပါ။ | ... pày·ba |
| bill | ဘောက်ချာ | bow'·cha |
| menu | မီးနူး | mì·nù |
| that dish | အဲ့ဒီ ဟင်းခွက် | è·di hìng·gwe' |
| wine list | ဝိုင်စာရင်း | waing·suh·yìng |

| (cup of ) coffee/tea | ကော်ဖီ/လက်ဖက်ရည် (၁ခွက်) | kaw·pi/luh·pe'·yay (tuh·kwe') |
| (mineral) water | ရေ(သန့်,ဖူး) | yay(·dháng·bòo) |
| glass of (wine) | (ဝိုင်) ၁ခွက် | (waing) tuh·kwe' |
| bottle of (beer) | (ဘီယာ) ၁ပုလင်း | (bi·ya) duh·buh·lìng |

| breakfast | မနက်စာ | muh·ne'·sa |
| lunch | နေ့လည်စာ | náy·le·za |
| dinner | ညစာ | nyá·za |

*Burmese*

18

# exploring

| | | |
|---|---|---|
| **Where's the ...?** | --- ဘယ်မှာလဲ။ | ... be·hma·lè |
| **bank** | ဘဏ်တိုက် | bang·dai' |
| **hotel** | ဟိုတယ် | hoh·te |
| **post office** | စာတိုက် | sa·dai' |
| **Where can I find ...?** | --- ဘယ်မှာ ရှိသလဲ။ | ... be·hma shí·dhuh·lè |
| **clubs** | ကလပ်တွေ | kuh·la'·tway |
| **pubs** | အရက်ဆိုင်တွေ | uh·ye'·şaing·dway |
| **restaurants** | စားသောက်ဆိုင်တွေ | sà·thow'·şaing·dway |

**Can you show me (on the map)?**
(မြေပုံပေါ်မှာ) ညွှန်ပြပေးပါ။ — (myay·bohng·baw·hma) hnyung·pyá·pày·ba

**What time does it open/close?**
ဘယ်အချိန် ဖွင့်/ပိတ်သလဲ။ — be·uh·chayng pwíng/pay'·dhuh·lè

**What's the admission charge?**
ဝင်ကြေး ဘယ်လောက်လဲ။ — wing·jày be·low'·lè

**When's the next tour?**
နောက်တသုတ် ဘယ်အချိန် စမလဲ။ — now'·tuh·thoh' be·uh·chayng sá·muh·lè

**Where can I buy a ticket?**
လက်မှတ် ဘယ်မှာ ဝယ်ရမလဲ။ — le'·hma' be·hma we·yá·muh·lè

| | | |
|---|---|---|
| **One ... ticket to (Taunggyi), please.** | (တောင်ကြီး) --- လက်မှတ် တစ်စောင် ပေးပါ။ | (towng·jì) ... le'·hma' duh·zowng pày·ba |
| **one-way** | အသွား | uh·thwà |
| **return** | အသွား အပြန် | uh·thwà uh·pyang |
| **My luggage has been ...** | ကျနော့်/ကျမ သေတ္တာ --- | chuh·náw/chuh·má thi'·ta ... m/f |
| **lost** | ပျောက်နေတယ် | pyow'·nay·de |
| **stolen** | ခိုးခံရတယ် | kòh·kang·yá·de |
| **Is this the ... to (Moulmein)?** | ဒါ (မော်လမြိုင်) သွားတဲ့ --- လား။ | da (maw·luh·myaing) thwà·dé ... là |
| **bus** | ဘတ်စကား | ba'·suh·kà |
| **plane** | လေယာဉ် | lay·ying |
| **train** | ရထား | yuh·tà |

Burmese

| | | |
|---|---|---|
| **What time's the … bus?** | --- ဘတ်စကား ဘယ်အချိန် ထွက်မလဲ။ | … ba'·suh·kà be·uh·chayng twe'·muh· |
| **first** | ပထမ | puh·tuh·má |
| **last** | နောက်ဆုံး | now'·şòhng |
| **next** | နောက် | now' |

| | | |
|---|---|---|
| **I'd like a taxi …** | --- တက္ကစီ လိုချင်ပါတယ်။ | … te'·kuh·si loh·jing·ba·de |
| **at (9am)** | (မနက် ၉နာရီ)မှာ | (muh·ne' kòh·na·yi)· |
| **tomorrow** | မနက်ဖြန် | muh·ne'·pang |

**How much is it to …?**
--- ကို ဘယ်လောက်လဲ။ … koh be·low'·lè

**Please put the meter on.**
မီတာ စမှတ်ပါ။ mi·ta sá·hma'·ba

**Please take me to (this address).**
(ဒီလိပ်စာ)ကို ပို့ပေးပါ။ (di·lay'·sa)·goh póh·pày·ba

**Please stop here.**
ဒီမှာ ရပ် ပါ။ di·hma ya' ba

# shopping

**Where's the (market)?**
(ဈေး) ဘယ်မှာလဲ။ (zày) be·hma·lè

**How much is it?**
ဒါ ဘယ်လောက်လဲ။ da be·low'·lè

**Can you write down the price?**
ဈေး ချရေးပေးပါ။ zày chá·yày·pày·ba

**That's too expensive.**
ဈေးကြီးလွန်းတယ်။ zày·chì·lùng·de

**There's a mistake in the bill.**
ဒီပြေစာမှာ အမှား ပါနေတယ်။ di·pyay·za·hma uh·hmà pa·nay·de

| | | |
|---|---|---|
| **It's faulty.** | ပျက်နေတယ်။ | pye'·nay·de |
| **I'd like a refund.** | ပိုက်ဆံ ပြန်အမ်းပါ။ | pai'·şang pyang·àng·ba |
| **I'd like to return this.** | ဒါ ပြန်ပေးချင်ပါတယ်။ | da pyang·pày·jing·ba·de |

| | | |
|---|---|---|
| **I'd like …, please.** | --- လိုချင်ပါတယ်။ | … loh·jing·ba·de |
| **my change** | ကျနော့်/ကျမ အကြွေ | chuh·náw/chuh·má uh·chway **m/f** |
| **a receipt** | ဘောက်ချာ | bow'·cha |

| | | |
|---|---|---|
| **Do you accept ...?** | --- လက်ခံသလား။ | ... le'·kang·dhuh·là |
| **credit cards** | ခရက်ဒစ်ကဒ် | kuh·ye'·di'·ka' |
| **travellers cheques** | ခရီးချက်လက်မှတ် | kuh·yì che'·le'·hma' |

# working

| | | |
|---|---|---|
| **I'm attending a ...** | --- လာ တက်တာ။ | ... la·te'·ta |
| **conference** | ညီလာခံ | nyi·la·gang |
| **course** | သင်တန်း | thing·dàng |
| **meeting** | အစည်းအဝေး | uh·sì·uh·wày |
| **I'm here for ...** | ဒီမှာ --- နေမှာ။ | di·hma ... nay·hma |
| **(two) days** | (နှစ်)ရက် | (hnuh)·ye' |
| **(three) weeks** | (သုံး)ပတ် | (thòhng)·buh' |
| **I'm with ...** | --- နဲ့ အတူတူ လာတာ။ | ... né uh·too·doo la·da |
| **my colleagues** | လုပ်ဖော်ကိုင် ဘက်တွေ | loh'·paw·kaing· be'·tway |
| **(two) others** | တခြား(နှစ်)ယောက် | tuh·chà·(hnuh)·yow' |

**I'm alone.**

| | |
|---|---|
| ကျနော်/ကျမ တစ်ယောက်တည်းပါ။ | chuh·naw/chuh·má tuh·yow'·tè·ba **m/f** |

**I'm staying at the (Thamada Hotel), room (28).**

| | |
|---|---|
| အခု (သမတ ဟိုတယ်) အခန်းနံပါတ်(၂၈) မှာ တည်းပါတယ်။ | uh·gú (thuh·muh·dá hoh·te) uh·kàng·nuhng·buh' (hnuh·şé·shi') hma tè·ba·de |

**I have an appointment with ...**

| | |
|---|---|
| --- နဲ့ ချိန်းထားတယ်။ | ... né chàyng·tà·de |

**Where's the conference/meeting?**

| | |
|---|---|
| ညီလာခံ/အစည်းအဝေး က ဘယ်မှာလဲ။ | nyi·la·gang/uh·sì·uh·wày gá be·hma·lè |

| | | |
|---|---|---|
| **I need ...** | --- လိုပါတယ်။ | ... loh·ba·de |
| **a computer** | ကွန်ပြူတာ | kung·pyoo·ta |
| **an internet connection** | အင်တာနက် ချိတ်ဖို့ | ing·ta·ne' chay'·póh |
| **an interpreter** | စကားပြန် | zuh·guh·byuhng |
| **to send a fax** | ဖက်စ်ပို့ဖို့ | faks·póh·bóh |

| Here's my ... | ဒီမှာ ကျွန်တော်/ကျွန်မ | di·hma chuh·náw/chuh·m |
| | --- ပါ။ | ... ba m/f |
| business card | လိပ်စာကဒ်ပြား | lay'·sa·kuh'·pyà |
| fax number | ဖက်စ် နံပါတ် | faks nuhng·buh' |
| mobile number | ဟင်းဖုန်း နံပါတ် | hìng·pòhng nuhng·bu |
| pager number | ပေဂျာ နံပါတ် | pay·ja nuhng·buh' |
| work number | အလုပ် ဖုန်းနံပါတ် | uh·loh' pòhng·nuhng· |

## Can I have your business card?

| ခင်ဗျား/ရှင်ရဲ့ လိပ်စာကဒ်ပြား | kuhng·myà/shíng·yé lay'·sa·kuh'·pyà |
| ပေးနိုင်မလား။ | pày·naing·muh·là m/f |

## That went very well.

| သိပ်ကောင်းတာပဲ။ | thay'·kòwng·da·bè |

## Thank you for your time.

| ကျေးဇူး တင်ပါတယ်။ | chày·zoo ting·ba·deh |

## Shall we go for a drink/meal?

| တခုခု သွားသောက်/သွားစား | tuh·kú·qú thwà·thow'/thwà·sà |
| ရအောင်။ | yá·owng |

## It's on me.

| ကျွန်တော်/ကျွန်မ ရှင်းလိုက်မယ်။ | chuh·naw/chuh·má shìng·lai'·me m/f |

# emergencies

| Help! | ကယ်ပါ။ | ke·ba |
| Stop! | ရပ်ပါ။ | ya'·pa |
| Go away! | သွား။ | thwà |
| Thief! | သူ့ခိုး။ | thuh·kòh |
| Fire! | မီး။ | mì |

| Call ...! | --- ခေါ်ပေးပါ။ | ... kaw·pày·ba |
| an ambulance | လူနာတင်ယာဉ် | loo·na·ting·ying |
| a doctor | ဆရာဝန် | şuh·ya·wung |
| the police | ပုလိပ် | puh·lay' |

## Could you help me, please?

| ကျေးဇူးပြုပြီး ကူညီပါ။ | chày·zù·pyú·pì koo·nyi·ba |

## I'm lost.

| လမ်းပျောက်နေတယ်။ | làng·pyow'·nay·de |

## Where are the toilets?

| အိမ်သာ ဘယ်မှာလဲ။ | ayng·dha be·hma·lè |

Burmese

# Cantonese

Get flummoxed and fired up in Hong Kong, a place born out of the clash and the confluence of China, Asia and the West.

# Pronunciation

| Vowels | | Consonants | |
|---|---|---|---|
| **Symbol** | **English sound** | **Symbol** | **English sound** |
| a | run | b | bed |
| aa | father | ch | cheat |
| aai | aisle (long) | d | dog |
| aau | now (long) | f | fat |
| ai | aisle (short) | g | go |
| au | now (short) | h | hat |
| aw | law | j | joke |
| ay | say | k | kit |
| e | bet | l | lot |
| eu | nurse | m | man |
| eui | eu followed by i | n | not |
| ew | i pronounced with rounded lips | ng | ring |
| i | see | p | pet |
| iu | youth | s | sun |
| o | note | t | top |
| oy | toy | w | win |
| u | put | y | yes |
| ui | with | | |

In Cantonese, the sound ng (found in English at the end or in the middle of words, eg 'ringing') can appear at the start of words. Note that words ending with the sounds p, t and k must be clipped – eg in English the p sound is much shorter in 'tip' than in 'pit'. Each syllable is separated by a dot, for example dàw·je. For **tones**, see page 12.

# essentials

| | | |
|---|---|---|
| Yes. | 係。 | haih |
| No. | 唔係。 | ǹg·haih |
| Hello. | 哈佬。 | hàa·ló |
| Goodbye. | 再見。 | joy·gin |
| Please ... | 唔該…… | ǹg·gòy ... |
| Thank you (very much). | 多謝(你)。 | dàw·je (láy) |
| You're welcome. | 唔駛客氣。 | ǹg·sái haak·hay |
| Excuse me./Sorry. | 對唔住。 | deui·ǹg·jew |
| Do you speak (English)? | 你識唔識講(英文)啊？ | láy sìk·ǹg·sìk gáwng (yìng·mán) aa |
| Do you understand? | 你明唔明啊？ | láy mìng·ǹg·mìng aa |
| I (don't) understand. | 我(唔)明。 | ngáw (ǹg) mìng |

# chatting

## introductions

| Mr/Ms | 先生／小姐 | ·sìn·sàang／·siú·jé |
|---|---|---|
| Mrs | 太太 | ·taai·táai |

**How are you?**
你幾好啊嗎？     láy gáy hó à maa

**Fine. And you?**
幾好。你呢？     gáy hó láy lè

**What's your name?**
你叫乜嘢名？     láy giu màt·yé méng aa

**My name is ...**
我叫……     ngáw giu ...

**I'm pleased to meet you.**
幸會！     hang·wui

**I'd like to introduce you to ...**
介紹……你識。     gaai·siu ... láy sìk

25

| Here's my ... | 呢個係我 | làygaw hai ngáw |
| | 嘅…… | ge ... |
| What's your ...? | 你嘅……呢？ | láy ge ... lè |
| address | 地址 | dayjí |
| email address | 電子郵箱 | dinjí yàusèung |
| phone number | 電話號碼 | dinwáa homáa |
| What's your occupation? | 你做邊行㗎？ | láy jo bìn hàwng gaa |
| I'm a ... | 我係…… | ngáw hai ... |
| businessperson | 生意人 | sàangyiyàn |
| student | 學生 | hawksàang |

**Where are you from?**
你係邊度人？　　　　láy hai bìndo yàn

**I'm from (England).**
我係喺(英國)嚟嘅。　ngáw hai hái (yìnggawk) lài ge

**Are you married?**
你係唔係結咗婚啊？　láy hainghai gitjáwfàn aa

| I'm ... | 我…… | ngáw ... |
| married | 結咗婚 | gitjáwfàn |
| single | 單身 | dàansàn |

**How old are you?**
你幾大啊？　　　　　láy gáy daai aa

**I'm ... years old.**
我……歲。　　　　　ngáw ... seui

## making conversation

**What's the weather like?**
天氣點樣？　　　　　tìnhay dímyéung

| It's ... | 天氣…… | tìnhay ... |
| cold | 凍 | dung |
| hot | 熱 | yit |
| raining | 落雨 | lawk yéw |
| snowing | 落雪 | lawk sewt |

**Do you live here?**
你住呢度啊？　　　　　láy jew lày·d<u>o</u> àa

**What are you doing?**
你做緊乜嘢？　　　　　láy jo·gán màt·yé

## meeting up

**What time will we meet?**
幾點見？　　　　　　　gáy dím gin

**Where will we meet?**
喺邊度見？　　　　　　hái bìn·d<u>o</u> gin

**Let's meet at ...**　　　我地喺……見。　ngáw·day hái ... gin
　**(eight) o'clock**　　（八）點鐘　　(baat) dím·jùng
　**the entrance**　　　門口　　　　　mùn·háu

**It's been great meeting you.**
識倒你真係好高興。　　sìk·dó láy jàn·hai hó gò·hing

# I love it here!
# 我鍾意呢度！
ngáw chùng·yi lày·d<u>o</u>

**Cantonese**

## likes & dislikes

| | | |
|---|---|---|
| **I thought it was ...** | 我以為佢…… | ngáw yí·wài kéui ... |
| **It's ...** | 佢…… | kéui ... |
| awful | 好差 | hó jáa |
| great | 好精彩 | hó jìng·chóy |
| interesting | 好得意 | hó dàk·yi |
| **Do you like ...?** | 你鍾唔鍾意……啊？ | láy jùng·ǹg·jùng yi ... aa |
| **I (don't) like ...** | 我（唔）鍾意…… | ngáw (ǹg·)jùng·yi ... |
| art | 藝術 | ngai·seut |
| sport | 體育 | tái·yuk |

27

# eating & drinking

| I'd like ..., please. | 唔該我要…… | ǹg·gòy ngáw yiu ... |
|---|---|---|
| the nonsmoking section | 不吸煙嘅檯 | bàt·kàp·yìn ge tóy |
| the smoking section | 吸煙嘅檯 | kàp·yìn ge tóy |
| a table for (five) | (五位)嘅檯 | (ńg wái) ge tóy |

**Do you have vegetarian food?**
有冇齋食品？  yáu·mó jàai sīk·bán

**What would you recommend?**
有乜嘢好介紹？  yáu màt·yé hó gaai·siu

## Would you like a drink?
### 你想飲啲乜嘢呢？
láy séung yám dì màt·yé lè

| I'll have a ... | 我要…… | ngáw yiu ... |
|---|---|---|
| Cheers! | 乾杯！ | gàwn·bùi |
| I'll have that. | 我點呢味。 | ngáw dím lày máy |

| I'd like the..., please. | 唔該我要…… | ǹg·gòy ngáw yiu ... |
|---|---|---|
| bill | 埋單 | màai·dàan |
| drink list | 酒料單 | jáu·liú·dàan |
| menu | 菜單 | choy·dàan |

| (cup of ) coffee/tea | (一杯)咖啡／茶 | (yàt bùi) gaa·fè/chàa |
|---|---|---|
| (mineral) water | (礦泉) 水 | (kawng·chèwn·)séui |
| glass of (wine) | 一杯 (葡萄酒) | yàt bui (pò·tò·jáu) |
| bottle of (beer) | 一樽 (啤酒) | yàt jèun (bè·jáu) |

| breakfast | 早餐 | jó·chàan |
|---|---|---|
| lunch | 午餐 | ńg·chàan |
| dinner | 晚飯 | máan·fāan |

Cantonese

# exploring

| Where's the ...? | ……喺邊度？ | ... hái·bìn·do |
|---|---|---|
| bank | 銀行 | ngàn·hàwng |
| hotel | 酒店 | jáu·dim |
| post office | 郵局 | yàu·gúk |

| Where can I find ...? | 邊度有……？ | bìn·do yáu ... |
|---|---|---|
| bars | 酒吧 | jáu·bàa |
| clubs | 夜總會 | ye·júng·wúi |
| restaurants | 酒樓 | jáu·làu |

**Can you show me (on the map)?**
你可唔可以（喺地圖度）指俾我睇我喺邊度？
láy háw·ǹg·háw·yí (hái day·tò do) jí báy ngáw tái ngáw hái bìn·do

**What time does it open/close?**
幾點開／關門？
gáy dím hòy/gwàan·mùn

**What's the admission charge?**
入場券幾多錢？
yap·chèung· gewn gáy·dàw chín

**When's the next tour?**
下個旅遊團係幾時？
haa·gaw léui·yàu·tèwn hai gáy·sì

**Where can I buy a ticket?**
去邊度買飛？
heui bìn·do máai fày

| One ... ticket to (Panyu), please. | 一張去（番禺）嘅……飛。 | yàt jèung heui (pùn·yèw) ge ... fày |
|---|---|---|
| one-way | 單程 | dàan·chìng |
| return | 雙程 | sèung·chìng |

| My luggage has been ... | 我嘅行李…… | ngáw ge hàng·láy ... |
|---|---|---|
| lost | 唔見咗 | ǹg·gin·jáw |
| stolen | 俾人偷咗 | báy·yàn tàu·jáw |

| Is this the ... to (Guangzhou)? | 呢班……係唔係去（廣州）㗎？ | lày bàan ... hai·ǹg·hai heui (gwáwng·jàu) gaa |
|---|---|---|
| bus | 巴士 | bàa·sí |
| plane | 飛機 | fày·gày |
| train | 火車 | fáw·chè |

Cantonese

29

Cantonese

| What time's the ... bus? | ⋯⋯巴士幾點開？ | ... bàa·sí gáy dím hòy |
| first | 頭班 | tàu·bàan |
| last | 尾班 | máy·bàan |
| next | 下一班 | haa·yàt·bàan |

**I'd like a taxi at (9am).**
我想（9點鐘）坐的士
ngáw séung (gáu dím·jùng) cháw dìk·sí

**I'd like a taxi tomorrow.**
我想坐的士听日
ngáw séung cháw dìk·sí tìng·yat

**How much is it to ...?**
去⋯⋯幾多錢？
heui ... gáy·dàw chín

**Please put the meter on.**
唔該打咪表。
ǹg·gòy dáa mài·bìu

**Please take me to (this address).**
唔該帶我去（呢個地址）。
ǹg·gòy daai ngáw heui (lày gaw day·jí)

**Please stop here.**
唔該喺呢度停。
ǹg·gòy hái lày·do tìng

# shopping

| Where's the (market)? | (街市)喺邊度？ | gàai·sí (hái·bìn·do) |
| How much is it? | 幾多錢？ | gáy·dàw chín |
| Can you write down the price? | 唔該寫低個价錢。 | ǹg·gòy sé dài gaw gaa·chìn |
| That's too expensive. | 太貴啦。 | taai gwai laa |
| There's a mistake in the bill. | 帳單錯咗。 | jeung·dàan chaw jáw |
| It's faulty. | 壞咗。 | waai·jáw |
| Could I have a receipt, please? | 唔該俾張單我。 | ǹg·gòy báy jèung dàan ngáw |

| I'd like ..., please. | 唔該，我要⋯⋯ | ǹg·gòy ngáw yiu ... |
| my change | 找錢 | jáau·chín |
| a refund | 退錢 | teui·chín |
| to return this | 退番呢個 | teui·fàan lày gaw |

30

| Do you accept ...? | 你地收唔收 | láy·day sàu·ǹg·sàu |
| | ······呀？ | ... aa |
| credit cards | 信用卡 | seun·yung·kàat |
| travellers cheques | 旅行支票 | léui·hàng jì·piu |

# working

| I'm attending a ... | 我參加個······ | ngáw chàam·gàa gaw ... |
| conference | 研討會 | yìn·tó·wúi |
| course | 培訓班 | puj·fan·bàan |
| meeting | 會議 | wúi·yí |
| trade fair | 交易會 | gàau·yjk·wúi |

| I'm here for ... | 我要住······ | ngáw yiu jew ... |
| (two) days | (二) 天 | (yị) yat |
| (four) weeks | (四) 個星期 | (say) gaw sìng·kày |

| I'm with ... | 我同······ | ngáw tung ... |
| | 一齊嚟嘅。 | yàt·chài lai ge |
| my colleague(s) | (幾個) 同事 | (gáy gaw) tung·sị |
| (two) others | (兩個) 人 | (léung gaw) yàn |

**I'm alone.**
我一個人嚟嘅。 ngáw yàt gaw yàn lại ge

**I have an appointment with ...**
我約咗······ ngáw yeuk·jáw ...

**I'm staying at the (China Hotel), room (100).**
我住喺 (中國大 ngáw jew hái (jùng·gawk daai
酒店), (一百) 房。 jáu·dim), (yàt·baak) fáwng

| Where's the ...? | ······喺邊度？ | ... hái·bìn·dọ |
| business centre | 商務中心 | sèung·mọ jùng·sàm |
| conference | 研討會 | yìn·tó·wúi |
| meeting | 會議 | wúi·yí |

| I need ... | 我要······ | ngáw yiu ... |
| a computer | 個電腦 | gaw dịn·lọ́ |
| an internet connection | 上網 | séung·máwng |
| an interpreter | 位翻譯 | wái fàan·yjk |
| to send a fax | 發個傳真 | faat gaw chẹwn·jàn |

31

| | | |
|---|---|---|
| **Here's my ...** | 俾我嘅……你。 | báy ngáw ge ... láy |
| business card | 卡片 | kàat·pín |
| fax number | 傳真號碼 | chèwn·jàn ho·máa |
| mobile number | 手機號碼 | sáu·gày ho·máa |
| pager number | 傳呼機號碼 | chèwn·fù·gày ho·máa |
| work number | 公司電話 | gùng·sì dìn·wáa |

**Can I have your business card?**
你有冇卡片呀？ — láy yáu·mó kàat·pín aa

**That went very well.**
會開得好好。 — wúi hòy dàk hó·hó

**Thank you for your time.**
唔該晒。 — ǹg·gòy saai

**Shall we go for a drink/meal?**
我地去飲杯／
食飯呢？ — ngáw·day heui yám·bùi/
sik·fàan lè

**It's on me.**
我請客。 — ngáw chéng haak

# emergencies

| | | |
|---|---|---|
| **Help!** | 救命！ | gau·meng |
| **Stop!** | 企喺度！ | káy hái·do |
| **Go away!** | 走開！ | jáu·hòy |
| **Thief!** | 有賊啊！ | yáu cháat aa |
| **Fire!** | 火燭啊！ | fó·jùk aa |

| | | |
|---|---|---|
| **Call ...!** | 快啲叫……！ | faai·dì giu ... |
| an ambulance | 救傷車 | gau·sèung·chè |
| a doctor | 醫生 | yì·sàng |
| the police | 警察 | gíng·chaat |

**Could you help me, please?**
唔該幫幫忙。 — ǹg·gòy bàwng bàwng màwng

**I'm lost.**
我蕩失路。 — ngáw dawng·sàk·lo

**Where are the toilets?**
廁所喺邊度？ — chi·sáw hái bìn·do

# Indonesian

Indonesia is where you can taste Southeast Asia's spicy melange — sample heady scents, vivid colours, dramatic vistas and diverse cultures.

# Pronunciation

| Vowels | | Consonants | |
|--------|---------------|------------|---------------|
| Symbol | English sound | Symbol | English sound |
| a | father | b | bed |
| ai | aisle | ch | cheat |
| e | bet | d | stop |
| ee | see | f | fat |
| ey | they | g | go |
| i | hit | h | hat |
| o | pot | j | joke |
| oo | zoo | k | kit |
| ow | how | kh | as the 'ch' in the Scottish *loch* |
| | | l | lot |
| | | m | man |
| | | n | not |
| | | ng | ring |
| | | ny | canyon |
| | | p | pet |
| | | r | red |
| | | s | sun |
| | | sh | shot |
| | | t | top |
| | | w | win |
| | | y | yes |

In Indonesian, the sound ng (found in English at the end or in the middle of words such as 'ringing') can also appear at the start of words. Note that in the combination ng·g, the second g is also pronounced, like in the word 'English' – eg *punggung* poong·goong (back).

The sounds r (rolled) and kh (guttural) are pronounced more distinctly than in English.

Each syllable is separated by a dot, for example si·la·kan.

Indonesian

34

# essentials

| | | |
|---|---|---|
| Yes./No. | *Ya./Tidak.* | ya/ti·dak |
| Hello. | *Salam.* | sa·lam |
| Goodbye. (leaving) | *Selamat tinggal.* | se·la·mat ting·gal |
| Goodbye. (staying) | *Selamat jalan.* | se·la·mat ja·lan |
| Please. | *Silakan.* | si·la·kan |
| Thank you | *Terima kasih* | te·ri·ma ka·sih |
| (very much). | *(banyak).* | (ba·nyak) |
| You're welcome. | *Kembali.* | kem·ba·li |
| Excuse me. | *Permisi.* | per·mi·si |
| Sorry. | *Maaf.* | ma·af |

**Do you speak (English)?**
*Anda bisa Bahasa (Inggris)?* — an·da bi·sa ba·ha·sa (ing·gris)

**Do you understand?**
*Anda mengerti?* — an·da meng·er·ti

**I (don't) understand.**
*Saya (tidak) mengerti.* — sa·ya (ti·dak) meng·er·ti

# chatting

## introductions

| | | |
|---|---|---|
| Mr | *Bapak* | ba·pak |
| Mrs/Miss | *Ibu/Nona* | i·boo/no·na |

**How are you?**
*Apa kabar?* — a·pa ka·bar

**Fine. And you?**
*Kabar baik. Anda bagaimana?* — ka·bar ba·ik an·da ba·gai·ma·na

**What's your name?**
*Siapa namanya?* — si·a·pa na·ma·nya

**My name is ...**
*Nama saya ...* — na·ma sa·ya ...

**I'm pleased to meet you.**
*Saya senang bertemu* — sa·ya se·nang ber·te·moo
*dengan Anda.* — deng·an an·da

| Here's my ... | Ini ... saya. | i·ni ... sa·ya |
| What's your ...? | Apa ... Anda? | a·pa ... an·da |
| address | alamat | a·la·mat |
| email address | alamat email | a·la·mat i·mel |
| phone number | nomor telpon | no·mor tel·pon |

| What's your occupation? | Pekerjaan Anda apa? | pe·ker·ja·an an·da a·pa |

| I'm a ... | Saya ... | sa·ya ... |
| businessperson | pedagang | pe·da·gang |
| student | mahasiswa | ma·ha·sis·wa |

**Where are you from?**
Anda dari mana? — an·da da·ri ma·na

**I'm from (England).**
Saya dari (Inggris). — sa·ya da·ri (ing·gris)

**Are you married (yet)?**
Sudah kawin? — soo·dah ka·win

**Not yet.**
Belum. — beo·loom

| I'm ... | Saya ... | sa·ya ... |
| married | sudah kawin | soo·dah ka·win |
| single | bujang | boo·jang |

**How old are you?**
Berapa umur Anda? — be·ra·pa oo·moor an·da

**I'm ... years old.**
Umur saya ... tahun. — oo·moor sa·ya ... ta·hoon

## making conversation

**What's the weather like?**
Cuacanya bagaimana? — choo·a·cha·nya ba·gai·ma·na

| It's ... | | |
| cloudy | Berawan. | be·ra·wan |
| cold | Dingin. | ding·in |
| hot | Panas. | pa·nas |
| raining | Hujan. | hoo·jan |
| windy | Berangin. | be·rang·in |

**Where do you live?**
*Anda tinggal di mana?*     an·da ting·gal di ma·na

**What are you doing?**
*Anda sedang melakukan apa*     an·da se·dang me·la·koo·kan a·pa

## meeting up

**What time will we meet?**
*Jam berapa kita jumpa?*     jam be·ra·pa ki·ta joom·pa

**Where will we meet?**
*Di mana kita jumpa?*     di ma·na ki·ta joom·pa

| | | |
|---|---|---|
| **Let's meet at …** | *Mari kita jumpa …* | ma·ri ki·ta joom·pa … |
| **(eight) o'clock** | *pada jam (delapan)* | pa·da jam (de·la·pan) |
| **the entrance** | *di pintu masuk* | di pin·too ma·sook |

**It's been great meeting you.**
*Saya senang bertemu*     sa·ya se·nang ber·te·moo
*dengan Anda.*     deng·an an·da

# I love it here!
## *Saya senang di sini!*
sa·ya se·nang di si·ni

## likes & dislikes

| | | |
|---|---|---|
| **I thought it was …** | *Saya pikir itu …* | sa·ya pi·kir i·too … |
| **It's …** | *Itu …* | i·too … |
| **awful** | *mengerikan* | meng·e·ri·kan |
| **great** | *jago* | ja·go |
| **interesting** | *menarik* | me·na·rik |
| | | |
| **Do you like …?** | *Anda suka …?* | an·da soo·ka … |
| **I (don't) like …** | *Saya (tidak) suka …* | sa·ya (ti·dak) soo·ka … |
| **art** | *seni* | se·ni |
| **sport** | *olahraga* | o·lah·ra·ga |

# eating & drinking

I'd like ..., please. | Saya minta ... | sa·ya min·ta ...
the nonsmoking section | tempat yang bebas asap rokok | tem·pat yang be·bas a·sap ro·kok
the smoking section | tempat yang boleh merokok | tem·pat yang bo·leh me·ro·kok
a table for (five) | meja untuk (lima) orang | me·ja oon·took (li·ma) o·rang

**Do you have vegetarian food?**
*Anda punya masakan khusus untuk vegetarian?*
an·da poo·nya ma·sa·kan khoo·soos oon·took ve·je·ta·ri·an

**What would you recommend?**
*Apa yang Anda rekomendasikan?*
a·pa yang an·da re·ko·men·da·si·kan

## Would you like a drink?
### *Mau minum?*
mow mi·noom

I'll have ... | Saya mau ... | sa·ya mow ...
Cheers! | Bersulang! | ber·soo·lang

I'd like (the) ..., please. | Saya minta ... | sa·ya min·ta ...
bill | kuitansi | koo·i·tan·si
drink list | daftar minuman | daf·tar mi·noo·man
menu | daftar makanan | daf·tar ma·ka·nan
that dish | hidangan itu | hi·dang·an i·too

(cup of) coffee/tea | (secangkir) kopi/teh | (se·chang·kir) ko·pi/teh
(mineral) water | air (mineral) | a·ir (mi·ne·ral)
glass of (wine) | segelas (anggur) | se·ge·las (ang·goor)
bottle of (beer) | satu botol (bir) | sa·too bo·tol (bir)

breakfast | sarapan | sa·ra·pan
lunch | makan siang | ma·kan si·ang
dinner | makan malam | ma·kan ma·lam

Indonesian

# exploring

| Where's the ...? | Di mana ...? | di ma·na ... |
|---|---|---|
| bank | bank | bank |
| hotel | hotel | ho·tel |
| post office | kantor pos | kan·tor pos |

| Where can I find ...? | Di mana saya dapat ...? | di ma·na sa·ya da·pat ... |
|---|---|---|
| bars | bar | bar |
| clubs | klub | kloob |
| restaurants | restoran | res·to·ran |

**Can you show me (on the map)?**
*Bisa tunjukkan kepada saya (di peta)?*
bi·sa toon·joo·kan ke·pa·da sa·ya (di pe·ta)

**What time does it open/close?**
*Jam berapa buka/tutup?*
jam be·ra·pa boo·ka/too·toop

**What's the admission charge?**
*Ongkos masuk berapa?*
ong·kos ma·sook be·ra·pa

**When's the next tour?**
*Kapan tour yang berikutnya?*
ka·pan toor yang be·ri·koot·nya

**Where can I buy a ticket?**
*Di mana saya bisa beli tiket?*
di ma·na sa·ya bi·sa be·li ti·ket

| One ... ticket (to Medan). | Satu tiket ... (ke Medan). | sa·too ti·ket ... (ke me·dan) |
|---|---|---|
| one-way | sekali jalan | se·ka·li ja·lan |
| return | pulang-pergi | poo·lang·per·gi |

| My luggage has been ... | Bagasi saya ... | ba·ga·si sa·ya ... |
|---|---|---|
| lost | hilang | hi·lang |
| stolen | dicuri | di·choo·ri |

| Is this the ... to (Ketapang)? | Ini ... yang ke (Ketapang)? | i·ni ... yang ke (ke·ta·pang) |
|---|---|---|
| boat | kapal | ka·pal |
| bus | bis | bis |
| train | kereta api | ke·re·ta a·pi |

Indonesian

| | | |
|---|---|---|
| **What time's the ... bus?** | *Jam berapa bis ...?* | jam be·ra·pa bis ... |
| first | *pertama* | per·ta·ma |
| last | *terakhir* | te·ra·khir |
| next | *yang berikutnya* | yang be·ri·koot·nya |

| | | |
|---|---|---|
| **I'd like a taxi ...** | *Saya mau taksi ...* | sa·ya mow tak·si ... |
| at (9am) | *pada (jam sembilan pagi)* | pa·da (jam sem·bi·lan pa·gi) |
| tomorrow | *besok* | be·sok |

**How much is it to (block M)?**
*Berapa ongkosnya kalau sampai (Blok M)?*
be·ra·pa ong·kos·nya ka·low sam·pai (blok em)

**Please put the meter on.**
*Tolong, pakai argo.*
to·long pa·kai ar·go

**Please take me to (this address).**
*Tolong antar saya ke (alamat ini).*
to·long an·tar sa·ya ke (a·la·mat i·ni)

**Please stop here.**
*Tolong berhenti di sini.*
to·long ber·hen·ti di si·ni

# shopping

**Where's the (market)?**
*Di mana (pasar)?*
di ma·na (pa·sar)

**How much is it?**
*Berapa harganya?*
be·ra·pa har·ga·nya

**Can you write down the price?**
*Bisa tulis berapa harganya?*
bi·sa too·lis be·ra·pa har·ga·nya

**That's too expensive.**
*Itu terlalu mahal.*
i·too ter·la·loo ma·hal

**There's a mistake in the bill.**
*Ada yang salah di bonnya.*
a·da yang sa·lah di bon·nya

**It's faulty.**
*Ini rusak.*
i·ni roo·sak

**Could I have a receipt, please?**
*Tolong, saya minta kuitansi.*
to·long sa·ya min·ta koo·i·tan·si

| I'd like ..., please. | Saya mau ... | sa·ya mow ... |
| my change | uang kembalian saya | oo·ang kem·ba·li·an sa·ya |
| a refund | uang saya kembali | oo·ang sa·ya kem·ba·li |
| to return this | kembalikan ini | kem·ba·li·kan i·ni |
| | | |
| Do you accept ...? | Anda menerima ...? | an·da me·ne·ri·ma ... |
| credit cards | kartu kredit | kar·too kre·dit |
| travellers cheques | cek perjalanan | chek per·ja·la·nan |

# working

| I'm attending a ... | Saya menghadiri ... | sa·ya meng·ha·di·ri ... |
| Where's the ...? | Di mana ...? | di ma·na ... |
| conference | konferensi | kon·fe·ren·si |
| course | kursus | koor·soos |
| meeting | rapat | ra·pat |
| trade fair | pekan raya dagang | pe·kan ra·ya da·gang |
| | | |
| I'm here for ... | Saya di sini selama ... | sa·ya di si·ni se·la·ma ... |
| (two) days | (dua) hari | (doo·a) ha·ri |
| (three) weeks | (tiga) minggu | (ti·ga) ming·goo |
| | | |
| I'm with ... | Saya dengan ... | sa·ya deng·an ... |
| my colleague(s) | teman sekerja saya | te·man se·ker·ja sa·ya |
| (two) others | (dua) orang lain | (doo·a) o·rang la·in |

**I'm alone.**
*Saya sendiri.*  sa·ya sen·di·ri

**I have an appointment with ...**
*Saya ada janji dengan ...*  sa·ya a·da jan·ji deng·an ...

**I'm staying at the (Hotel Ayu), room (14).**
*Saya tinggal di (Hotel Ayu),*  sa·ya ting·gal di (ho·tel a·yoo)
*kamar nomor (empatbelas).*  ka·mar no·mor (em·pat·be·las)

| I need ... | Saya perlu ... | sa·ya per·loo ... |
| a computer | komputer | kom·poo·ter |
| an internet connection | koneksi internet | ko·nek·si in·ter·net |
| an interpreter | juru bahasa | joo·roo ba·ha·sa |
| to send a fax | kirim faks | ki·rim faks |

41

| Here's my ... | Ini ... saya. | i·ni ... sa·ya |
| business card | kartu nama | kar·too na·ma |
| fax number | nomor faks | no·mor faks |
| mobile number | nomor HP | no·mor ha·pe |
| pager number | nomor pager | no·mor pe·jer |
| work number | nomor telpon | no·mor tel·pon |
| | kantor | kan·tor |

**Can I have your business card?**
*Boleh minta kartu nama Anda?* bo·leh min·ta kar·too na·ma an·da

**That went very well.**
*Itu berjalan baik.* i·too ber·ja·lan ba·ik

**Thank you for your time.**
*Terima kasih atas waktunya.* te·ri·ma ka·sih a·tas wak·too·nya

**Shall we go for a drink/meal?**
*Mau pergi minum/* mow per·gi mi·noom/
*makan bersama?* ma·kan ber·sa·ma

**It's on me.**
*Saya traktir.* sa·ya trak·tir

# emergencies

| Help! | Tolong! | to·long |
| Stop! | Berhenti! | ber·hen·ti |
| Go away! | Pergi! | per·gi |
| Thief! | Pencuri! | pen·choo·ri |
| Fire! | Api! | a·pi |

| Call ...! | Panggil ...! | pang·gil ... |
| an ambulance | ambulansi | am·boo·lan·si |
| a doctor | dokter | dok·ter |
| the police | polisi | po·li·si |

**Could you help me, please?**
*Bisa Anda bantu saya?* bi·sa an·da ban·too sa·ya

**I'm lost.**
*Saya tersesat.* sa·ya ter·se·sat

**Where are the toilets?**
*Di mana kamar kecil?* di ma·na ka·mar ke·chil

# Japanese

Surf an indoor wave, muse in a Zen temple, take a kip in a capsule – are you ready to be surprised?

# Pronunciation

| Vowels | | Consonants | |
|---|---|---|---|
| Symbol | English sound | Symbol | English sound |
| a | run | b | bed |
| ā | father | ch | cheat |
| ai | aisle | d | stop |
| air | fair | f | fat (almost like 'fw', with rounded lips) |
| e | bet | g | go (hard) |
| ē | reign | h | hat |
| i | hit | j | joke |
| ī | see | k | kit |
| o | pot | m | man |
| ō | law | n | not |
| ow | how | p | pet |
| oy | toy | r | red (halfway between 'r' and 'l') |
| u | put | s | sun |
| ū | zoo | sh | shot |

In Japanese, vowel length can change the meaning of a word. The long vowel sounds should be held twice as long as the short ones and are represented in our pronunciation guides with a horizontal line on top (eg ū). It's also important to make the distinction between single and double consonants. Say the double consonants with a slight pause between them – eg sak·ka (writer). Each syllable is separated by a dot, for example a·ri·ga·tō.

| | |
|---|---|
| t | top |
| ts | hats |
| w | win |
| y | yes |
| z | zero |

Japanese

# essentials

| | | |
|---|---|---|
| Yes. | はい。 | hai |
| No. | いいえ。 | i·e |
| Hello. | こんにちは。 | kon·ni·chi·wa |
| Goodbye. | さようなら。 | sa·yō·na·ra |
| Please. (asking) | ください。 | ku·da·sai |
| Please. (offering) | どうぞ。 | dō·zo |
| Thank you (very much). | (どうも)ありがとう (ございます)。 | (dō·mo) a·ri·ga·tō (go·zai·mas) |
| You're welcome. | どういたしまして。 | dō i·ta·shi·mash·te |
| Excuse me. | すみません。 | su·mi·ma·sen |
| Sorry. | ごめんなさい。 | go·men·na·sai |
| Do you speak English? | 英語が話せますか? | ē·go ga ha·na·se·mas ka |
| Do you understand? | わかりましたか? | wa·ka·ri·mash·ta ka |
| I understand. | わかりました。 | wa·ka·ri·mash·ta |
| I don't understand. | わかりません。 | wa·ka·ri·ma·sen |

# chatting

## introductions

| | | |
|---|---|---|
| Mr/Mrs/Miss ... | ...さん | ...·san |

**How are you?**
お元気ですか?    o·gen·ki des ka

**Fine. And you?**
はい、元気です。    hai gen·ki des
あなたは?    a·na·ta wa

**What's your name?**
お名前は何ですか?    o·na·ma·e wa nan des ka

**My name is ...**
私の名前は...です。    wa·ta·shi no na·ma·e wa ... des

**I'm pleased to meet you.**
お会いできてうれしいです。    o·ai de·ki·te u·re·shī des

45

| Here's my ... | これが私の…です。 | ko·re ga wa·ta·shi no ... des |
| What's your ...? | あなたの…は何ですか? | a·na·ta no ... wa nan des ka |
| address | 住所 | jū·sho |
| email address | Eメールアドレス | i·mē·ru·a·do·res |
| phone number | 電話番号 | den·wa·ban·gō |

| What's your occupation? | お仕事は何ですか? | o·shi·go·to wa nan des ka |

| I'm a ... | 私は…です。 | wa·ta·shi wa ... des |
| businessperson | ビジネスマン | bi·ji·nes·man |
| student | 生徒 | sē·to |

**Where are you from?**

| どちらから来ましたか? | do·chi·ra ka·ra ki·mash·ta ka |

**I'm from (England).**

| (イギリス)から来ました。 | (i·gi·ri·su) ka·ra ki·mash·ta |

**Are you married?**

| 結婚していますか? | kek·kon shi·te i·mas ka |

| I'm ... | 私は… | wa·ta·shi wa ... |
| married | 結婚しています | kek·kon shi·te i·mas |
| single | 独身です | do·ku·shin des |

**How old are you?**

| おいくつですか? | oy·ku·tsu des ka |

**I'm ... years old.**

| 私は…歳です。 | wa·ta·shi wa ... sai des |

## making conversation

**What's the weather like?**

| 天気はどうですか? | ten·ki wa dō des ka |

| It's ... | …です。 | ... des |
| cold | 寒い | sa·mu·i |
| hot | 暑い | a·tsu·i |
| raining | 雨 | a·me |
| snowing | 雪 | yu·ki |

**Do you live here?**
ここに住んでいますか?  ko·ko ni sun·de i·mas ka

**What are you doing?**
何をしていますか?  na·ni o shi·te i·mas ka

## meeting up

**What time will we meet?**
何時に会いましょうか?  nan·ji ni ai·ma·shō ka

**Where will we meet?**
どこで会いましょうか?  do·ko de ai·ma·shō ka

**Let's meet at ...**  …会いましょう。  ... ai·ma·shō
  **(eight) o'clock**  (8)時に  (ha·chi)·ji ni
  **the entrance**  入口で  i·ri·gu·chi de

**It's been great meeting you.**
あなたに会えてとても  a·na·ta ni a·e·te to·te·mo
よかったです。  yo·kat·ta des

# I love it here!
ここが大好きです!
ko·ko ga dai·su·ki des

## likes & dislikes

**I thought it was ...**  …と思いました。  ... to o·moy·mash·ta
**It's ...**  …です。  ... des
  **awful**  ひどい  hi·doy
  **great**  素晴らしい  su·ba·ra·shī
  **interesting**  面白い  o·mo·shi·roy

**Do you like ...?**  …が好きですか?  ... ga su·ki des ka
**I like ...**  …が好きです。  ... ga su·ki des
**I don't like ...**  …が好きじゃ  ... ga su·ki ja
ありません。  a·ri·ma·sen
  **art**  美術  bi·ju·tsu
  **sport**  スポーツ  spō·tsu

47

# eating & drinking

| I'd like ..., please. | …をお願いします。 | ... o o·ne·gai shi·mas |
|---|---|---|
| the nonsmoking section | 禁煙席 | kin·en·se·ki |
| the smoking section | 喫煙席 | ki·tsu·en·se·ki |
| a table for (five) | (5)人分の テーブル | (go)·nim·bun no tē·bu·ru |

**I don't eat meat.**

肉は食べません。　　　　　ni·ku wa ta·be·ma·sen

**What would you recommend?**

なにがおすすめですか?　　na·ni ga o·su·su·me des ka

## Would you like a drink?
### 何か飲みませんか?
na·ni ka no·mi·ma·sen ka

| I'll have a ... | …をお願いします。 | ... o o·ne·gai shi·mas |
|---|---|---|
| Cheers! | 乾杯! | kam·pai |
| I'll have that. | あれをください。 | a·re o ku·da·sai |

| I'd like the ..., please. | …をお願いします。 | ... o o·ne·gai shi·mas |
|---|---|---|
| bill | 勘定 | kan·jō |
| drink list | 飲み物の メニュー | no·mi·mo·no no me·nyū |
| menu | メニュー | me·nyū |

| (cup of) coffee/tea | コーヒー/紅茶(1杯) | kō·hī/kō·cha (ip·pai) |
|---|---|---|
| mineral water | ミネラルウォーター | mi·ne·ra·ru·wō·tā |
| water | 水 | mi·zu |
| bottle of (beer) | (ビール)を大ビンで | (bī·ru) o ō·bin de |
| glass of (wine) | (ワイン)をグラスで | (wain) o gu·ra·su de |

| breakfast | 朝食 | chō·sho·ku |
|---|---|---|
| lunch | 昼食 | chū·sho·ku |
| dinner | 夕食 | yū·sho·ku |

# exploring

| Where's the...? | ...はどこですか? | ... wa do·ko des ka |
|---|---|---|
| bank | 銀行 | gin·kō |
| hotel | ホテル | ho·te·ru |
| post office | 郵便局 | yū·bin·kyo·ku |

| Where can I find ...? | どこに行けば ...がありますか? | do·ko ni i·ke·ba ... ga a·ri·mas ka |
|---|---|---|
| clubs | クラブ | ku·ra·bu |
| pubs | パブ | pa·bu |
| restaurants | レストラン | res·to·ran |

**Can you show me (on the map)?**
(地図で)教えて
くれませんか?
(chi·zu de) o·shi·e·te
ku·re·ma·sen ka

**What time does it open?**
何時に開きますか?
nan·ji ni a·ki·mas ka

**What time does it close?**
何時に閉まりますか?
nan·ji ni shi·ma·ri·mas ka

**What's the admission charge?**
入場料はいくらですか?
nyū·jō·ryō wa i·ku·ra des ka

**When's the next tour?**
次のツアーはいつですか?
tsu·gi no tsu·ā wa i·tsu des ka

**Where can I buy a ticket?**
切符はどこで買えますか?
kip·pu wa do·ko de ka·e·mas ka

| One ... ticket (to Tokyo). | (東京行きの) ...切符。 | (tō·kyō·yu·ki no) ... kip·pu |
|---|---|---|
| one-way | 片道 | ka·ta·mi·chi |
| return | 往復 | ō·fu·ku |

| My luggage has been ... | 私の 手荷物が... | wa·ta·shi no te·ni·mo·tsu ga ... |
|---|---|---|
| lost | なくなりました | na·ku·na·ri·mash·ta |
| stolen | ぬすまれました | nu·su·ma·re·mash·ta |

| Is this the ... to (Kobe)? | (神戸)行きの... はこれですか? | (kō·be)·yu·ki no ... wa ko·re des ka |
|---|---|---|
| boat | 船 | fu·ne |
| bus | バス | bas |
| train | 電車 | den·sha |

| What time's the ... bus? | ...バスは 何時ですか? | ... bas wa nan·ji des ka |
|---|---|---|
| first | 始発の | shi·ha·tsu no |
| last | 最終の | sai·shū no |
| next | 次の | tsu·gi no |

| I'd like a taxi ... | ...タクシーを お願いします。 | ... tak·shī o o·ne·gai shi·mas |
|---|---|---|
| at (9) o'clock | (9)時に | (ku)·ji ni |
| tomorrow | 明日 | a·shi·ta |

**How much is it to ...?**
...までいくらですか?  ... ma·de i·ku·ra des ka

**Please put the meter on.**
メーターを入れてください。  mē·tā o i·re·te ku·da·sai

**Please take me to (this address).**
(この住所) まで
お願いします。  (ko·no jū·sho) ma·de o·ne·gai shi·mas

**Please stop here.**
ここで停まってください。  ko·ko de to·mat·te ku·da·sai

# shopping

**Where's the (market)?**
《市場》はどこですか?  (i·chi·ba) wa do·ko des ka

**How much is it?**
いくらですか?  i·ku·ra des ka

**Can you write down the price?**
値段を書いてもらえますか?  ne·dan o kai·te mo·ra·e·mas ka

**That's too expensive.**
高すぎます。  ta·ka·su·gi·mas

**There's a mistake in the bill.**
請求書に間違いがあります。  sē·kyū·sho ni ma·chi·gai ga a·ri·mas

**It's faulty.**
不良品です。  fu·ryō·hin des

| I'd like ..., please. | ...をお願いします。 | ... o o·ne·gai shi·mas |
|---|---|---|
| my change | お釣り | o·tsu·ri |
| a receipt | レシート | re·shī·to |
| a refund | 払い戻し | ha·rai·mo·do·shi |
| to return this | 返品 | hem·pin |

| | | |
|---|---|---|
| **Do you accept ...?** | …で支払えますか？ | ... de·shi·ha·ra·e·mas ka |
| credit cards | クレジットカード | ku·re·jit·to·kā·do |
| travellers | トラベラーズ | to·ra·be·rāz· |
| cheques | チェック | chek·ku |

# working

| | | |
|---|---|---|
| **I'm attending a ...** | …に出席します。 | ... ni shus·se·ki shi·mas |
| conference | 会議 | kai·gi |
| course | コース | kōs |
| meeting | ミーティング | mī·tin·gu |
| trade fair | 展示会 | ten·ji·kai |
| **I'm here for ...** | 私は… | wa·ta·shi wa ... |
| | 滞在します。 | tai·zai shi·mas |
| ... days | …日 | ...·ni·chi |
| ... weeks | …年 | ...·nen |
| **I'm with ...** | …といっしょです。 | ... to is·sho des |
| my colleague(s) | 同僚 | dō·ryō |
| (two) others | ほかの（2人） | ho·ka no (fu·ta·ri) |

**I'm alone.**
私は1人です。 wa·ta·shi wa hi·to·ri des

**I have an appointment with ...**
…とアポがあります。 ... to a·po ga a·ri·mas

**I'm staying at the ..., room ...**
…の…号室に ... no ...·go·shi·tsu ni
泊まっています。 to·mat·te i·mas

| | | |
|---|---|---|
| **Where's the ...?** | …はどこですか？ | ... wa do·ko des ka |
| business centre | ビジネスセンター | bi·ji·nes·sen·tā |
| conference | 会議 | kai·gi |
| meeting | ミーティング | mī·tin·gu |
| **I need ...** | …が必要です。 | ... ga hi·tsu·yō des |
| a computer | コンピュータ | kom·pyū·ta |
| an internet | インターネットの | in·tā·net·to no |
| connection | 接続 | se·tsu·zo·ku |
| an interpreter | 通訳 | tsū·ya·ku |
| to send a fax | ファックス送信 | fak·kus·sō·shin |

| Here's my ... | これが私の…です。 | ko·re ga wa·ta·shi no ... |
| business card | 名刺 | mē·shi |
| fax number | ファックス番号 | fak·kus·ban·gō |
| mobile number | 携帯番号 | kē·tai·ban·gō |
| pager number | ポケベル番号 | po·ke·be·ru·ban·gō |
| work number | 仕事の | shi·go·to no |
| | 電話番号 | den·wa·ban·gō |

**Can I have your business card?**
あなたの名刺は何ですか？　　a·na·ta no mē·shi wa nan des ka

**That went very well.**
非常にうまくいきました。　　hi·jō ni u·ma·ku i·ki·ma·shi·ta

**Thank you for your time.**
お時間をどうもありがとう　　o·ji·kan o dō·mo a·ri·ga·tō
ございました。　　go·zai·mash·ta

**Shall we go for a drink?**
飲みに行きましょうか？　　sho·ku·ji ni i·ki·ma·shō ka

**Shall we go for a meal?**
食事に行きましょうか？　　no·mi ni i·ki·ma·shō ka

**It's on me.**
私のおごりです。　　wa·ta·shi no o·go·ri des

# emergencies

| Help! | たすけて！ | tas·ke·te |
| Stop! | 止まれ！ | to·ma·re |
| Go away! | 離れろ！ | ha·na·re·ro |
| Thief! | どろぼう！ | do·ro·bō |
| Fire! | 火事だ！ | ka·ji da |

| Call ...! | …を呼んで！ | ... o yon·de |
| an ambulance | 救急車 | kyū·kyū·sha |
| a doctor | 医者 | i·sha |
| the police | 警察 | kē·sa·tsu |

**Could you help me, please?**
たすけてください。　　tas·ke·te ku·da·sai

**I'm lost.**
迷いました。　　ma·yoy·mash·ta

**Where are the toilets?**
トイレはどこですか？　　toy·re wa do·ko des ka

# Khmer

Vibrant culture, charming people, jaw-dropping sights . . . Cambodia is kicking!

# Pronunciation

| Vowels | | Consonants | |
|---|---|---|---|
| **Symbol** | **English sound** | **Symbol** | **English sound** |
| a | calm (short) | b | bed |
| aa | calm (longer) | ɓ | puppy (hard) |
| aar | aa plus er | ch | cheat |
| aay | aisle (longer) | d | dog |
| ae | act | ɗ | stand (hard) |
| ai | aisle (short) | g | go |
| ao | how | h | hat |
| aw | saw | j | joke |
| ay | say | k | kit |
| e | bang | l | lot |
| ee | see | m | man |
| ee-aa | ee plus aa | n | not |
| ee-uh | ee plus uh | ng | ring |
| eh | say (short, hard) | ny | canyon |
| ei | uh plus ee | p | pet |
| er | jerk (soft, open) | r | red (hard, rolled) |
| eu | ee pronounced with rounded lips | s | sun |
| | | t | top |
| eu-uh | eu plus uh | w | win |
| euw | a very nasal eu | y | yes |
| ih | a short, hard ee | | |
| oh | note (short, hard) | | |
| oo | zoo | | |
| ooh | a short, hard ow | | |
| ow | glow (long) | | |
| u | Luke | | |
| uh | but | | |

Note that the ɓ sound is halfway between a 'b' and a 'p', and the ɗ sound is halfway between a 'd' and a 't'.

Each syllable is separated by a dot, for example nee·uhng.

Khmer

54

# essentials

| | | |
|---|---|---|
| Yes. (said by a man) | បាទ | baat |
| Yes. (said by a woman) | ចាស | jaa |
| No. | ទេ | đay |
| Hello. | ជំរាបសួរ | johm ree-uhp soo-uh |
| Goodbye. | លាសិនហើយ | lee-aa suhn hao-y |
| Please. | សូម | sohm |
| Thank you (very much). | អរគុណ (ច្រើន) | aw gohn (juh-rarn) |
| You're welcome. | មិនអីទេ | muhn ei đay |
| Excuse me./Sorry. | សុំទោស | sohm đoh |

**Do you speak English?**

អ្នកចេះភាសាអង់គ្លេសទេ?    nay-uhk jes phi-a-saa awn-glay đay

**Do you understand?**

អ្នកយល់ទេ?    nay-uhk yuhl đay

**I understand.**

ខ្ញុំយល់ហើយ    kuh-nyohm yuhl hao-y

**I don't understand.**

ខ្ញុំមិនយល់ទេ    kuh-nyohm muhn yuhl đay

# chatting

## introductions

| | | |
|---|---|---|
| Mr | លោក | lohk |
| Mrs | លោកស្រី | lohk srei |
| Ms | នាង | nee-uhng |

| | | |
|---|---|---|
| How are you? | សុខសប្បាយទេ? | sohk sa-baay đay |
| Fine. And you? | ខ្ញុំសុខសប្បាយ | kuh-nyohm sohk sa-baay |
| | ចុះអ្នក? | joh nay-uhk |
| What's your name? | អ្នកឈ្មោះអ្វី? | nay-uhk chuh-mu-ah ei |
| My name is ... | ខ្ញុំឈ្មោះ ... | kuh-nyohm chuh-mu-ah ... |
| I'm pleased to meet you. | ខ្ញុំរីករាយដោយ បានជួបអ្នក | kuh-nyohm reek ree-ay dao-y baan ju-uhp nay-uhk |

55

| Here's my ... | នេះជា ... ខ្ញុំ | nih jee·aa ... kuh·nyohm |
| What's your ...? | សុំ ... របស់អ្នក? | sohm ... ruh·bawh nay·u |
| address | អាសយដ្ឋាន | aa·sai·yah·taan |
| email address | អាស្រេសអ៊ីមែល | aa·dreh ee·mail |
| phone number | លេខទូរស័ព្ទ | layk đoo·rah·sahp |

| What's your occupation? | តើអ្នកធ្វើការអ្វី? | đaar nay·uhk twer gaa ah·wei |

| I'm a/an ... | ខ្ញុំធ្វើការជា ... | kuh·nyohm twer gaa jee· |
| office worker | បុគ្គលិកនៅ | bohk·ga·lerk neuw |
| | ការិយាល័យ | gaa·ree·aa·lai |
| student | និស្សិត | ni·suht |

| Where are you from? | អ្នកមកពីណា? | nay·uhk mao ƀee naa |
| I'm from (England). | ខ្ញុំមកពី | kuh·nyohm mao ƀee |
| | (អង់គ្លេស) | (awng·glay) |

| Are you married? | អ្នកមានគ្រួសារ | nay·uhk mee·uhn kru·ah |
| | ហើយឬនៅ? | saa hao·y reu neuw |

| I'm ... | ខ្ញុំ ... | kuh·nyohm ... |
| married | មានគ្រួសារហើយ | mee·uhn kru·ah saa h |
| single | នៅលីវ | neuw liw |

| How old are you? | | |
| អ្នកអាយុប៉ុន្មាន? | | nay·uhk aa·yuh ƀohn·maan |
| I'm ... years old. | | |
| ខ្ញុំអាយុ ... ឆ្នាំ | | kuh·nyohm aa·yooh ... chuh·nuhm |

## making conversation

**What's the weather like?**

ធាតុអាកាសយ៉ាងម៉េចទៅ? tee·uht·aa·kah yahng mait đeuw

| It's ... | វា ... | wee·aa ... |
| cold | ត្រជាក់ | đraw·jay·uhk |
| (very) hot | ក្តៅ (ណាស់) | guh·daa·ew (nah) |
| rainy | ភ្លៀង | plee·uhng |
| warm | កក់ក្តៅ | gawk guh·daa·ew |

56

**Do you live here?**
អ្នកនៅទីនេះឬ? nay·uhk neuw tee nih reuh

**What are you doing?**
អ្នកកំពុងធ្វើអីហ្ន៎ង? nay·uhk kam·pong twer ei neung

**I love it here!**
ខ្ញុំចូលចិត្តទីនេះណាស់! kuh·nyohm johl juht tee nih

## meeting up

**What time will we meet?**
យើងជួបគ្នាម៉ោងប៉ុន្មាន? yeung joob kuh·neer maong pon maan

**Where will we meet?**
យើងជួបគ្នានៅទីណា? yeung joob kuh·neer neuw tee naa

| | | |
|---|---|---|
| Let's meet at ... | អីចឹងជួប | ee jeung joob |
| | គ្នានៅ ... | kuh·neer neuw ae ... |
| (eight) o'clock | ម៉ោង (ប្រាំបី) | maong (bram bei) |
| the entrance | ច្រកចូល | chrawk johl or pleuw johl |

It's been great ជាការប្រសើរណាស់ jee·aa gaa praw·saar nas
meeting you. ដែលបានជួបអ្នក del baan joob nay·uhk

## likes & dislikes

| | | |
|---|---|---|
| I thought it was ... | ខ្ញុំគិតថាវាជា ... | kuh·nyohm kuht tha wee·aa jee·aa ... |
| It's ... | វាគី ... | wee·aa keu ... |
| awful | មិនល្អសោះ | muhn la·aw soh |
| great | ល្អណាស់ | la·aw nas |
| interesting | គួរឲ្យចាប់ | goo·uh ao·y jarb |
| | អារម្មណ៍មែន | aa·ruhm men |

| | | |
|---|---|---|
| Do you like ...? | តើអ្នកចូលចិត្ត | đaar nay·uhk johl juht |
| | ... ទេ? | ... đay |
| I (don't) like ... | ខ្ញុំ (មិន) | kuh·nyohm (muhn) |
| | ចូលចិត្ត ... (ទេ) | johl juht ... (đay) |
| art | សិល្បៈ | sil·a·bah |
| sport | កីឡា | gei·laa |

57

Khmer

# eating & drinking

| | | |
|---|---|---|
| I'd like ..., please. | ខ្ញុំសុំ ... | kuh·nyohm sohm ... |
| the (non)smoking | កន្លែងក្នែង | đohk neuw guhn·lain |
| section | (មិន) ឲ្យជក់បារី | (muhn) ao·y joo·uhk b |
| a table for (four) | តុសំរាប់ | đohk suhm·rahp |
| | (បួន) នាក់ | (boo·uhn) nay·uhk |

**Do you have vegetarian food?**

ទីនេះមានឧបករម្ភូប
đee nih mee·uhn lu·uhk
បួសទេ?
muh·howp bu·uh đay

**Would you like a drink?**

តើអ្នកចង់ញ៉ាំភេសជ្ជៈទេ?    daar nay·uh jawng nyam phe·sa·jaa

| | | |
|---|---|---|
| I'll have ... | ខ្ញុំសុំ ... | kuh·nyohm sohm ... |
| Cheers! | ជំយោ! | chuh·yow |

| | | |
|---|---|---|
| I'd like ..., please. | សុំ ... | sohm ... |
| the bill | គិតលុយ | kuht luy |
| the menu | ម៉ឺនុយ | me·nuy |
| that dish | មុខម្ហូបនោះ | mohk muh·howp nuh |

| | | |
|---|---|---|
| (cup of) coffee/tea | កាហ្វេ/តែ (មួយពែង) | gaa·fay/đai (muy beng) |
| (mineral) water | ទឹក (មានាតពុះ) | đuhk (mee·uhn bo·buh) |
| glass of (wine) | (ស្រាទំពាំងបាយជូរ) | (sraa đohm·bay·uhng |
| | មួយកែវ | baay joo) muy gaiw |
| bottle of (beer) | (បៀរ) មួយដប | (bee·ah) muy dawp |

| | | |
|---|---|---|
| breakfast | អ្ហូបពេលព្រឹក | muh·howp behl bruhk |
| lunch | អ្ហូបថ្ងៃត្រង់ | muh·howp tuh·ngai đraw |
| dinner | អ្ហូបពេលល្ងាច | muh·howp behl luh·ngee |

# exploring

| | | |
|---|---|---|
| Where's the ...? | ... នៅឯណា? | ... neuw ei naa |
| bank | ធនាគារ | tuh·nee·ah·gee·aa |
| hotel | សណ្ឋាគារ | suhn·taa·gee·aa |
| post office | ប្រៃសណីយ៍ | prai·suh·nee |

**Khmer**

| | | |
|---|---|---|
| **Where are the ...?** | មាន ... នៅឯណា? | mee·uhn ... neuw ei naa |
| clubs | កន្លែងដីស្គ | guhn·laing dis·kow |
| restaurants | រោងនីយដ្ឋាន | pow·chuh·nee·yuh·taan |

**Can you show me (on the map)?**
សុំបង្ហាញខ្ញុំ (លើផែនទី)
sohm bawng·hain kuh·nyohm
(ler pain·dee)

**What time does it open/close?**
កន្លែងនេះបើក/ បិទ
ម៉ោងប៉ុន្មាន?
guhn·laing nih baok/buht
maong bohn·maan

**What's the admission charge?**
តំលៃចូលថ្លៃប៉ុន្មាន?
duhm·lai johl tuh·lai bohn·maan

**When's the next tour?**
ដើរទស្សនាទៅអង្កាល់?
daar đoh·sah·naa đeuw ahng·kahl

**Where can I buy a ticket?**
ខ្ញុំត្រូវទិញសំបុត្រ
នៅឯណា?
kuh·nyohm đrow đeen suhm·boht
neuw ei naa

| | | |
|---|---|---|
| **My luggage has been ...** | វ៉ាលិសរបស់ ខ្ញុំត្រូវ ... | waa·lih ruh·bawh kuh·nyohm đrow ... |
| lost | បាត់ | baht |
| stolen | គេលួច | gay loo·iht |

| | | |
|---|---|---|
| **One ... ticket to (Battambang), please.** | សុំសំបុត្រ ... មួយទៅ ( បាត់ដំបង) | sohm suhm·boht ... muy đeuw (baht·duhm·bawng) |
| one-way | តែទៅទេ | đai đeuw đay |
| return | ទៅមក | đeuw mao |

| | | |
|---|---|---|
| **Is this the ... to (Siem Reap)?** | នេះជា ... ទៅ (សៀមរាប) ទេ? | nih jee·aa ... đeuw (see·uhm ree·uhp) đay |
| bus | ឡានឈ្នួល | laan chuh·nool |
| plane | យន្តហោះ | yohn hawh |
| train | រថភ្លើង | rah·teh plerng |

| | | |
|---|---|---|
| **What time's the ... bus?** | ឡានឈ្នួល ... ចេញទៅម៉ោងប៉ុន្មាន? | laan chuh·nool ... jain đeuw maong bohn·maan |
| first | មុនគេបង្អស់ | mun gay bawng·awh |
| last | ចុងក្រោយបង្អស់ | johng krao·y bawng·awh |

**Khmer**

| I'd like a taxi ... | ខ្ញុំផ្លូវការរថយន្ត តាក់ស៊ី ... | kuh-nyohm đrow gaa la đahk-see ... |
| at (9am) | នៅម៉ោង (ប្រាំបួនព្រឹក) | neuw maong (bruhm boo-uhn bru... |
| tomorrow | ថ្ងៃស្អែក | tuh-ngai suh-aik |

**How much is it to ...?**

| ទៅ ... យកថ្លៃប៉ុន្មាន? | đeuw ... yohk tuh-lai bohn-maan |

**Please put the meter on.**

| សូមប្រើម៉ីរ័ដផង | sohm braar mee-đer pawng |

**Please take me to (this address).**

| សូមជូនខ្ញុំទៅ (អាសយដ្ឋាននេះ) | sohm jun kuh-nyohm đeuw (aa-sai-yah-tahn nih) |

**Please stop here.**

| សូមឈប់នៅទីនេះ | sohm chohp neuw đee nih |

# shopping

| Where's the (market)? | (ផ្សារ) នៅឯងណា? | (puh-saa) neuw ei naa |
| How much is it? | ថ្លៃប៉ុន្មាន? | tuh-lai bohn-maan |
| Can you write down the price? | សូមសរសេរ តំលៃ ឲ្យខ្ញុំ | sohm saw-say duhm-lai ao-y kuh-nyohm |
| That's too expensive. | ថ្លៃពេក | tuh-lai bayk |
| There's a mistake in the bill. | គិតលុយខុសហើយ | kuht luy koh hao-y |
| It's faulty. | វាខូចហើយ | wee-aa ko-iht hao-y |
| I'd like ..., please. | ខ្ញុំសុំ ... | kuh-nyohm sohm ... |
| my change | លុយអាប់របស់ខ្ញុំ | luy ahp ruh-bawh kuh... |
| a receipt | បង្កាន់ដៃ | bawng-guhn dai |
| a refund | ឲ្យប្រាក់សង | ao-y nay-uhk sawng |
| | តំលៃវិញ | duhm-lai wee-aa wei... |
| to return this | សងអីវាន់នេះវិញ | sawng ei-wuhn nih w... |
| Do you accept ...? | អ្នកទទួល ... បានទេ? | nay-uhk đoh-đool ... baan đay |
| credit cards | ប័ត្រក្រេឌីត | baht kre-điht |
| travellers cheques | សែកទេសចរ | saik đeh-sah-jaw |

60

# working

| | | |
|---|---|---|
| I'm attending a ... | ខ្ញុំកពុល្យម ... | kuh·nyohm mao jool roorm ... |
| conference | សន្និសីទ | suhn·nee·suht |
| course | វគ្គសិក្សា | wa·ak sik saa |
| meeting | កិច្ចប្រជុំ | kich pra·chum |
| trade fair | ពិព័រណ៍ផ្តព័រណ៍ | pee·thee tang pi·paw |
| | ពាណិជ្ជកម្ម | peer·nich·kam |
| I'm with ... | ខ្ញុំកជាមួយ ... | kuh·nyohm mao jeer muy ... |
| my colleagues | សហការីខ្ញុំ | sa·haak·kaa·rei |
| | | kuh·nyohm |
| (two) others | មនុស្ស (ពីរ) | mo·nuh (pee) |
| | នាក់ទៀត | nay·uhk teeh |

I'm here for (three) days/weeks.
ខ្ញុំនៅទីនេះរយៈពេល   kuh·nyohm neuw tee nih ro·yaak pel
(បី) ថ្ងៃ/អាទិត្យ   (bei) tuh·ngai/aa·tuht

I'm alone.
ខ្ញុំមកតែម្នាក់ឯងទេ   kuh·nyohm mao tae ma·nay·uhk aing teh

I have an appointment with ...
ខ្ញុំមានការណាត់   kuh·nyohm mee·uhn gaa nat
ជួបជាមួយ ...   joob muy ...

Where's the (business centre)?
តើ (មណ្ឌលពាណិជ្ជកម្ម)   daar (mon·dol peer nich·kam)
នៅទីណា?   neuw tee nah

| | | |
|---|---|---|
| I need ... | ខ្ញុំត្រូវការ ... | kuh·nyohm treuw gaa ... |
| a computer | កុំព្យូទ័រមួយ | kom·pyu·ter muy |
| an interpreter | អ្នកបកប្រែ | nay·uhk boork prae |
| | ភាសាម្នាក់ | pheer·saa ma·nah |
| to send a fax | ផ្ញើហ្វាក់ | puh·nyaar fahk |
| Here's my ... | នេះគឺជា ... | nih keur jeer ... |
| | របស់ខ្ញុំ | ruh·bawh kuh·nyohm |
| business card | កាតវីហ្ស៊ីត | gaat wee·zeet |
| fax number | លេខហ្វាក់ | layk fahk |
| pager number | លេខផេកជើរ | layk pay·jer |

Khmer

61

**Can I have your business card?**

ខ្ញុំអាចសុំកាតវិបហ្សិត
របស់អ្នកបានទេ?

kuh·nyohm aach sohm gaat
vee·zeet nay·uhk baan đay

**That went very well.**

អ្វីៗបានដំណើរការល្អ

ah·wei ah·wei baan dohm·neur kaa

**Thank you for your time.**

អរគុណចំពោះពេល
វេហារបស់អ្នក

aw·gun jom pos pel wel·leer
ruh·bawh nay·uhk

**Shall we go for a drink?**

តើយើងអាចទៅញ៉ាំ
គេសជ្ជៈបានទេ?

daar yeung aach teu nyuhm
phe·saa·jay·uhk baan đay

**Shall we go for a meal?**

តើយើងអាចទៅញ៉ាំ
អាហារបានទេ?

daar yeung aach teu nyuhm
a·haa baan đay

**It's on me.**

វាទៅនឹងខ្ញុំ

wee·aa neuw neung kuh·nyohm

# emergencies

| | | |
|---|---|---|
| **Help!** | ជួយផង! | joo·y pawng |
| **Stop!** | ឈប់! | chohp |
| **Go away!** | ទៅអោយឆ្ងាយ! | đeuw ao·y chuh·ngaay |
| **Thief!** | ចោរ! | jao |
| **Fire!** | ភ្លើងឆេះ! | plerng cheh |

| | | |
|---|---|---|
| **Call ...!** | ជួយហៅ ... មក! | joo·y haa·ew ... mao |
| an ambulance | ឡានពេទ្យ | laan baet |
| a doctor | គ្រូពេទ្យ | kru baet |
| the police | ប៉ូលិស | bow·lih |

**Could you help me, please?**

ជួយខ្ញុំផងបានទេ?

joo·y kuh·nyohm pawng baan đay

**I'm lost.**

ខ្ញុំវង្វេងផ្លូវ

kuh·nyohm wohng·weng pleuw

**Where are the toilets?**

បង្គន់នៅឯណា?

bawng·gohn neuw ei naa

62

# Korean

Korea is fast forward all the way —
a country of endless possibilities with
limits imposed only by you.

# Pronunciation

| Vowels | | Consonants | |
|--------|--------------|--------|--------------|
| Symbol | English sound | Symbol | English sound |
| a | father | b | bed |
| ae | bag | ch | cheat |
| e | net | ch' | cheat (aspirated) |
| o | go | d | dog |
| ŏ | son | g | go |
| oé | no entry (with a shortened 'o') | h | hat (aspirated) |
| u | nude | j | joke |
| ŭ | put | k | kit |
| üi | chop suey (with a shortened 'u') | k' | kit (aspirated) |
| i | keen | l | lot |
| | | m | man |
| | | n | not |
| | | ng | ring |
| | | p | pet |
| | | p' | pet (aspirated) |
| | | r | red |
| | | s | sun (aspirated) |
| | | sh | shot |
| | | t | top |
| | | t' | top (aspirated) |
| | | w | win |
| | | y | yes |

The pronunciation guide in this chapter is modelled on the so-called 'McCune-Reischauer' system of writing Korean using the Roman alphabet. Korean has aspirated consonants (pronounced with a puff of air after the sound) and unaspirated ones. The aspirated consonants (except for h and s) are followed by an apostrophe (') in our pronunciation guides. Note that double consonants are pronounced more quickly and forcefully than single consonants. When two particles are separated with a slash, the first one is used after a consonant and the second one after a vowel. Each syllable is separated by a dot, for example yŏ·gi·yo.

# essentials

| | | |
|---|---|---|
| Yes./No. | 네/아니오. | ne/a·ni·o |
| Hello. | 안녕하세요. | an·nyŏng·ha·se·yo |
| Goodbye. (staying) | 안녕히 가세요. | an·nyŏng·hi ka·se·yo |
| Goodbye. (leaving) | 안녕히 계세요. | an·nyŏng·hi kye·se·yo |
| Thank you (very much). | (정말) 고맙습니다. | (chŏng·mal) ko·map·sŭm·ni·da |
| You're welcome. | 천만에요. | ch'ŏn·ma·ne·yo |
| Excuse me. | 여기요. | yŏ·gi·yo |
| Sorry. | 죄송합니다. | choé·song·ham·ni·da |

**Do you speak English?**
영어 할줄 아시나요?　　　yŏng·ŏ hal·jul a·shi·na·yo

**Do you understand?**
알아 들으셨나요?　　　　　a·ra dŭ·rŭ·shŏss·ŏ·yo

**I (don't) understand.**
(못) 알아 들었어요.　　　　(mot) a·ra dŭ·rŏss·ŏ·yo

# chatting

## introductions

| | |
|---|---|
| Mr/Mrs/Miss ... 　　… 씨 | ... shi/ssi |

**How are you?**
안녕하세요?　　　　　　an·nyŏng·ha·se·yo

**Fine. And you?**
네. 안녕하세요?　　　　ne, an·nyŏng·ha·se·yo

**What's your name?**
성함을 여쭤봐도　　　　sŏng·ha·mŭl yŏt·chŏ·bwa·do
될까요?　　　　　　　　doélk·ka·yo

**My name is ...**
제 이름은 … 입니다.　　che i·rŭ·mŭn ... im·ni·da

**I'm pleased to meet you.**
만나서 반갑습니다.　　　man·na·sŏ pan·gap·sŭm·ni·da

| Here's my ... | 제 … 입니다. | che … im·ni·da |
|---|---|---|
| What's your ...? | 좀 … | chom … |
| | 알려주세요. | al·lyŏ·ju·se·yo |
| (email) address | (이메일) 주소 | (i·me·il) ju·so |
| phone number | 전화번호 | chŏn·hwa bŏn·ho |
| What's your occupation? | 무슨일 하세요? | mu·sŭ·nil ha·se·yo |
| I'm a ... | 저는 … 입니다. | chŏ·nŭn … im·ni·da |
| businessperson | 사업가 | sa·ŏp·ka |
| student | 학생 | hak·saeng |

**Where are you from?**
어느 나라에서 오셨어요?    ŏ·nŭ na·ra·e·sŏ o·shŏss·ŏ·yo

**I'm from (England).**
저는 (영국)에서
왔습니다.    chŏ·nŭn (yŏng·guk)·e·sŏ wass·sŭm·ni·da

**Are you married?**
결혼 하셨어요?    kyŏ·ron ha·shŏss·ŏ·yo

**I'm married/single.**
결혼 했어요/
미혼이에요.    kyŏ·ron haess·ŏ·yo/ mi·ho·ni·e·yo

**How old are you? (to someone younger/older)**
나이가 어떻게 돼요?    na·i·ga ŏt·tŏ·k'é twae·yo
연세가 어떻게 되세요?    yŏn·sé·ga ŏt·tŏ·k'é toé·se·yo

**I'm ... years old.**
저는 … 살입니다.    chŏ·nŭn … sa·rim·ni·da

## making conversation

**What's the weather like?**
날씨가 어때요?    nal·shi·ga ŏt·tae·yo

| It's cold. | 추워요. | ch'u·wŏ·yo |
| It's hot. | 더워요. | tŏ·wŏ·yo |
| It's raining. | 비가 와요. | pi·ga wa·yo |
| It's snowing. | 눈이 와요. | nu·ni wa·yo |

| Do you live here? | 여기 사시나요? | yŏ·gi sa·shi·na·yo |
| What are you doing? | 뭐 하세요? | mwŏ ha·se·yo |

## meeting up

**What time will we meet?**
우리 언제 만날까요? u·ri ŏn·jé man·nalk·ka·yo

**Where will we meet?**
어디에서 만날까요? ŏ·di·e·sŏ man·nalk·ka·yo

**Let's meet at ...** ··· 만나요. ... man·na·yo
  **(eight) o'clock** (여덟) 시에 (yŏ·dŏl) shi·é
  **the entrance** 입구에서 ip·ku·e·sŏ

**It's been great meeting you.**
만나서 반가웠습니다. man·na·sŏ pan·ga·wŏss·sŭm·ni·da

# I love it here!
# 여기 정말 좋아요!
## yŏ·gi chŏng·mal cho·a·yo

## likes & dislikes

**It is/was awful.**
끔찍해요/ ggŭm·tchi·k'ae·yo/
끔찍했어요. ggŭm·tchi·k'aess·ŏ·yo

**It is/was great.**
좋아요/좋았어요. cho·a·yo/cho·ass·ŏ·yo

**It is/was interesting.**
흥미로워요/ hŭng·mi·ro·wŏ·yo/
흥미로웠어요. hŭng·mi·ro·wŏss·ŏ·yo

**Do you like ...?** ··· 좋아 ... cho·a·
  하세요? ha·se·yo
**I like ...** 전 ···을/를 chŏn ...ŭl/·rŭl
  좋아해요. cho·a·hae·yo
**I don't like ...** 전 ···을/를 chŏn ...ŭl/·rŭl
  싫어해요. shi·rŏ·hae·yo

  **art** 미술 mi·sul
  **sport** 운동 un·dong

# eating & drinking

| I'd like ..., please. | … 부탁 합니다. | … pu·t'ak ham·ni·da |
|---|---|---|
| the nonsmoking section | 금연 구역 | kŭ·myŏn ku·yŏk |
| the smoking section | 흡연 구역 | hŭ·byŏn ku·yŏk |
| a table for (four) | (네) 명 앉을 테이블 | (ne) myŏng an·jŭl t'e·i·bŭl |

**Do you have vegetarian food?**
채식주의 음식 있나요?　　ch'ae·shik·ju·i ŭm·shik in·na·yo

**What's delicious here?**
여기 뭐가 맛있나요?　　yŏ·gi mwŏ·ga ma·shiss·ŏ·yo

## Would you like a drink?
음료수 드시겠어요?
ŭm·nyo·su dŭ·shi·gess·ŏ·yo

| I'll have a ... | … 주세요. | … ju·se·yo |
|---|---|---|
| Cheers! | 건배! | kŏn·bae |

| I'd like (the) ..., please. | … 주세요. | … ju·se·yo |
|---|---|---|
| bill | 계산서 | kye·san·sŏ |
| drink list | 음료수 메뉴 | ŭm·nyo·su me·nyu |
| menu | 메뉴 | me·nyu |
| that dish | 저 메뉴 | chŏ me·nyu |

| coffee/tea | 커피/차 | k'ŏ·p'i/ch'a |
|---|---|---|
| mineral water | 생수 | saeng·su |
| water | 물 | mul |
| glass of (wine) | (와인) 한잔 | (wa·in) han·jan |
| bottle of (beer) | (맥주) 한병 | (maek·chu) han·byŏng |

| breakfast | 아침 | a·ch'im |
|---|---|---|
| lunch | 점심 | chŏm·shim |
| dinner | 저녁 | chŏ·nyŏk |

Korean

# exploring

| | | |
|---|---|---|
| Where's the ...? | … 어디<br>있어요? | … ŏ·di<br>iss·ŏ·yo |
| bank | 은행 | ŭn·haeng |
| hotel | 호텔 | ho·t'el |
| post office | 우체국 | u·ch'e·guk |
| I want to<br>find ... | … 찾으려고<br>하는데요. | … ch'a·jŭ·ryŏ·go<br>ha·nŭn·de·yo |
| clubs | 클럽 | k'ŭl·lŏp |
| bars | 술집 | sul·chip |
| restaurants | 식당 | shik·tang |

**Can you show me (on the map)?**
(이 지도에서) 어디예요? (i ji·do·e·sŏ) ŏ·di·ye·yo

**What time does it open/close?**
언제 문 열어요/닫아요? ŏn·jé mun yŏ·rŏ·yo/ta·da·yo

**What's the admission charge?**
입장료가 얼마예요? ip·chang·nyo·ga ŏl·ma·ye·yo

**When's the next tour?**
다음 투어가 언제예요? ta·ŭm t'u·ŏ·ga ŏn·je·ye·yo

**Where can I buy a ticket?**
표 어디에서 사요? p'yo ŏ·di·e·sŏ sa·yo

| | | |
|---|---|---|
| One ... ticket<br>to (Wonju),<br>please. | (원주 가는)<br>…표 한장<br>주세요. | (wŏn·ju ka·nŭn)<br>…·p'yo han·jang<br>ju·se·yo |
| one-way | 편도 | p'yŏn·do |
| return | 왕복 | wang·bok |
| My luggage<br>has been ... | 제 짐이 … | che ji·mi ... |
| lost | 없어졌어요 | ŏp·sŏ·jŏss·ŏ·yo |
| stolen | 도난 당했어요 | to·nan dang·haess·ŏ·yo |
| Is this the ...<br>to (Gwangju)? | 이게 (광주)로<br>가는 …<br>인가요? | i·ge (kwang·ju)·ro<br>ka·nŭn ...<br>in·ga·yo |
| bus | 버스 | bŏ·sŭ |
| plane | 비행기 | pi·haeng·gi |
| train | 기차 | ki·ch'a |

| What time's the ... bus? | ... 버스 언제 있어요? | ... bŏ·sŭ ŏn·jé iss·ŏ·yo |
|---|---|---|
| first | 첫 | ch'ŏt |
| last | 마지막 | ma·ji·mak |
| next | 다음 | ta·ŭm |

| I'd like a taxi ... | ... 택시 부탁 드려요. | ... t'aek·shi pu·t'ak dŭ·ryŏ·yo |
|---|---|---|
| at (9am) | (오전 아홉 시)에 | (o·jŏn a·hop shi)·é |
| tomorrow | 내일 | nae·il |

**How much is it to ...?**
... 까지 얼마예요?     ... kka·ji ŏl·ma·ye·yo

**Please put the meter on.**
미터기 켜주세요.     mi·t'ŏ·gi k'yŏ·ju·se·yo

**Please take me to (Namdaemun).**
(남대문)으로 가주세요.     (nam·dae·mun)·ŭ·ro ka·ju·se·yo

**Please stop here.**
여기 내릴게요.     yŏ·gi nae·ril·ke·yo

# shopping

| Where's the (market)? | (시장이) 어디 있어요? | (shi·jang·i) ŏ·di iss·ŏ·yo |
|---|---|---|
| How much is it? | 얼마예요? | ŏl·ma·ye·yo |
| Can you write down the price? | 가격을 써 주시겠어요? | ka·gyŏ·gŭl ssŏ ju·shi·gess·ŏ·yo |
| That's too expensive. | 너무 비싸요. | nŏ·mu pi·ssa·yo |
| There's a mistake in the bill. | 계산서가 이상해요. | kye·san·sŏ·ga i·sang·hae·yo |
| It's faulty. | 불량이에요. | pul·lyang·i·e·yo |
| I'd like a refund. | 환불 하고 싶습니다. | hwan·bul ha·go ship·sŭm·ni·da |
| I'd like to return this. | 반품 하고 싶습니다. | pan·p'um ha·go ship·sŭm·ni·da |

| I'd like ..., please. | ... 주세요. | ... ju·se·yo |
|---|---|---|
| my change | 잔돈 | chan·don |
| a receipt | 영수증 | yŏng·su·jŭng |

70

| Do you accept ...? | … 받으시나요? | ... pa·dŭ·shi·na·yo |
| credit cards | 신용 카드 | shin·yong k'a·dŭ |
| travellers cheques | 여행자 수표 | yŏ·haeng·ja su·p'yo |

# working

| I'm attending<br>a ... | …에 참가 하고<br>있어요. | ...·e ch'am·ga ha·go<br>iss·ŏ·yo |
| conference | 회의 | hoé·i |
| course | 수업 | su·ŏp |
| meeting | 회의 | hoé·i |
| trade fair | 무역 박람회 | mu·yŏk pang·nam·hoé |

| I'm with ... | …와/과 같이<br>있어요. | ...·wa/·gwa ka·ch'i<br>iss·ŏ·yo |
| my colleagues | 제 동료들 | che dong·nyo·dŭl |
| (two) others | 다른 (두)명 | ta·rŭn (du)·myŏng |

**I'm alone.**
전 혼자예요.     chŏn hon·ja·ye·yo

**I'm here for (three) days/weeks.**
여기 (삼) 일/주     yŏ·gi (sam) il/ju
동안 있어요.     dong·an iss·ŏ·yo

**I have an appointment with ...**
…와/과 약속이 있어요.    ...·wa/·gwa yak·so·gi iss·ŏ·yo

| Where's the ...? | …이/가 어디<br>있어요? | ...·i/·ga ŏ·di<br>iss·ŏ·yo |
| business centre | 비즈니스<br>센터 | bi·jŭ·ni·sŭ<br>sen·t'ŏ |
| conference hall | 회의장 | hoé·i·jang |
| meeting hall | 회의장 | hoé·i·jang |

| I need ... | …이/가<br>필요 해요. | ...·i/·ga<br>p'i·ryo hae·yo |
| a computer | 컴퓨터 | k'ŏm·p'yu·t'ŏ |
| an internet<br>connection | 인터넷 연결 | in·t'ŏ·net yŏn·gyŏl |
| an interpreter | 통역사 | t'ong·yŏk·sa |

| I need to send<br>a fax. | 팩스를<br>보내야 해요. | p'aek·sŭ·rŭl<br>po·nae·ya hae·yo |

| Here's my ... | 제 … 입니다. | che ... im·ni·da |
|---|---|---|
| business card | 명함 | myŏng·ham |
| fax number | 팩스 번호 | p'aek·sŭ bŏn·ho |
| mobile number | 휴대폰 번호 | hyu·dae·p'on bŏn·ho |
| pager number | 호출기 번호 | ho·ch'ul·gi bŏn·ho |
| work number | 직장 번호 | chik·chang bŏn·ho |

**Can I have your business card?**
명함 부탁 드려도
될까요?
myŏng·ham pu·tak dŭ·ryŏ·do
doélk·ka·yo

**That went very well.**
정말 잘 되었어요.
chŏng·mal jal doé·ŏss·ŏ·yo

**Thank you for your time.**
시간 내주셔서
감사 합니다.
shi·gan nae·ju·shŏ·sŏ
kam·sa ham·ni·da

**Shall we go for a drink/meal?**
뭐 마시러/먹으러
갈까요?
mwŏ ma·shi·rŏ/mŏ·gŭ·rŏ
kalk·ka·yo

**It's on me.**
제가 살게요.
che·ga sal·ke·yo

# emergencies

| Help! | 도와주세요! | to·wa·ju·se·yo |
|---|---|---|
| Stop! | 멈추세요! | mŏm·ch'u·se·yo |
| Go away! | 저리 가세요! | chŏ·ri ka·se·yo |
| Thief! | 도둑이야! | to·du·gi·ya |
| Fire! | 불이야! | pu·ri·ya |

| Call ...! | … 불러주세요! | ... pul·lŏ·ju·se·yo |
|---|---|---|
| an ambulance | 구급차 | ku·gŭp·ch'a |
| a doctor | 의사 | ŭi·sa |
| the police | 경찰 | kyŏng·ch'al |

**Could you help me, please?**
좀 도와주시겠어요? chom to·wa·ju·shi·gess·ŏ·yo

**I'm lost.**
길을 잃었어요. ki·rŭl i·rŏss·ŏ·yo

**Where are the toilets?**
화장실이 어디예요? hwa·jang·shi·ri ŏ·di·ye·yo

# Lao

Laos – home of Southeast Asia's most pristine environment, intact cultures and quite possibly the most chilled-out people on Earth.

# Pronunciation

| Vowels | | Consonants | |
|--------|---------------|--------|---------------|
| **Symbol** | **English sound** | **Symbol** | **English sound** |
| a | **run** | b | **b**ed |
| aa | **act** | ɓ | s**p**in |
| aa-ou | **aa** followed by u | d | **d**og |
| ah | **father** | ɗ | s**t**op |
| ai | **aisle** (longer) | f | **f**at |
| air | **fair** | g | **g**o |
| e | **bed** | h | **h**at |
| ee | **see** | j | **j**oke |
| eu | **nurse** | k | **k**it |
| i | **hit** | l | **l**ot |
| o | **pot** | m | **m**an |
| oh | **note** | n | **n**ot |
| oo | **zoo** | ng | ri**ng** |
| or | **for** | ny | ca**ny**on |
| ow | **how** | p | **p**et |
| oy | **toy** | s | **s**un |
| u | **put** | t | **t**op |
| | | w | **w**in |
| | | y | **y**es |

In this chapter, we've used hyphens to separate syllables in a word (eg ang-gít), and further divided separate vowel sounds within the one syllable with a dot (eg kĕe·an).

The ɓ sound is halfway between a 'b' and a 'p', and the ɗ sound is halfway between a 'd' and a 't'.

For **tones**, see page 12.

# essentials

| | | |
|---|---|---|
| Yes./No. | ແມ່ນ/ບໍ່ | maan/bor |
| Hello. | ສະບາຍດີ | sa-bai dee |
| Goodbye. | ລາກ່ອນ | lah gorn |
| Please. | ກະລຸນາ | ga-lú-náh |
| Thank you. | ຂອບໃຈ | kòrp jai |
| You're welcome. | ດ້ວຍຄວາມຍິນດີ | doo-ay kwáhm nyeen dée |
| Excuse me./Sorry. | ຂໍໂທດ | kŏr-tòht |
| | | |
| Do you speak English? | ເຈົ້າເວົ້າພາສາອັງກິດໄດ້ບໍ່? | jôw wôw páh-săh àng-gít dâi bor |
| Do you understand? | ເຈົ້າເຂົ້າໃຈບໍ່? | jôw kôw jai bor |
| I (don't) understand. | ຂ້ອຍ (ບໍ່) ເຂົ້າໃຈ | kòy (bor) kôw-jai |

# chatting

## introductions

| | | |
|---|---|---|
| Mr | ທ່ານ | tahn |
| Mrs | ນາງ | náhng |
| Miss | ນາງສາວ | náhng sŏw |
| | | |
| How are you? | ເຈົ້າສະບາຍດີບໍ່? | jôw sa-bai dee bor |
| Fine. And you? | ສະບາຍດີເຈົ້າເດ? | sa-bai dee jôw dáir |
| What's your name? | ເຈົ້າຊື່ຫຍັງ? | jôw seu nyăng |
| My name is … | ຂ້ອຍຊື່ … | kòy seu … |
| I'm pleased to meet you. | ຍິນດີທີ່ໄດ້ຮູ້ຈັກ | nyín dée tee dâi hôo ják |
| | | |
| Here's my … | ນີ້ແມ່ນ … ຂອງຂ້ອຍ | nêe maan … kŏrng kòy |
| What's your …? | … ຂອງເຈົ້າແມ່ນຫຍັງ? | … kŏrng jôw maan nyăng |
| address | ທີ່ຢູ່ | tee yoo |
| email address | ອິແມວ | ée-máa-ou |
| phone number | ເບີໂທລະສັບ | beu tóh-la-sáp |

| What's your occupation? | ອາຊີບເຈົ້າເຮັດຫຍັງ? | ah-sêep jôw hét nyâng |
| I'm a/an ... | ຂ້ອຍເປັນ ... | kòy bén ... |
| office worker | ພະນັກງານ | pà-nak ngáhn |
| | ຫ້ອງການ | hòrng gahn |
| student | ນັກສຶກສາ | nak séuk-sǎh |

| Where are you from? | ເຈົ້າມາແຕ່ໃສ? | jôw mah đaa sǎi |
| --- | --- | --- |

| I'm from (England). | ຂ້ອຍເປັນຄົນ (ອັງກິດ) | kòy bén kón (àng-gít) |
| --- | --- | --- |

| Are you married? | ເຈົ້າແຕ່ງງານແລ້ວຫລືບໍ່? | jôw đaang ngáhn lâa-ou leu bor |
| --- | --- | --- |

| How old are you? | ເຈົ້າອາຍຸຈັກປີ? | jôw ah-nyù ják bee |
| I'm ... years old. | ຂ້ອຍອາຍຸ ... ປີ | kòy ah-nyu ... bee |

| I'm ... | ຂ້ອຍ ... | kòy ... |
| married | ແຕ່ງງານແລ້ວ | đaang ngáhn lâa-ou |
| single | ເປັນໂສດ | bén sôht |

## I love it here!
ຂ້ອຍມັກທີ່ນີ້
kòy mak tée nêe

Lao

# making conversation

**What's the weather like?**
ອາກາດເປັນຈັ່ງໃດ?
àh-gaht bèn jáng dai

**It's raining hard.**
ຝົນກຳລັງຕົກໜັກ
fǒn gam-lang đók nák

**It's (very) cold/hot.**
ມັນໜາວ/ຮ້ອນ (ຫລາຍ)
mán nǒw/hôrn (lǎi)

**Do you live here?**
ເຈົ້າພັກຢູ່ພີ້ບໍ່?
jôw pak yoo pêe bor

**What are you doing?**
ເຈົ້າເຮັດຫຍັງ?
jôw het nyǎng

76

## meeting up

**What time will we meet?**
ເຮົາຈະພົບກັນຈັກໂມງ?     hów já pop gan ják móhng

**Where will we meet?**
ເຮົາຈະພົບກັນຢູ່ໃສ?     hów já pop gan yoo săi

Let's meet at ...    ພົບກັນ ...     pop gan ...
   (eight) o'clock    (ແປດ) ໂມງ     (ɓáad) móhng
   the entrance    ຢູ່ທາງເຂົ້າ     yoo táhng kòw

**It's been great meeting you.**
ດີໃຈທີ່ໄດ້ພົບກັນ     dee jai tée dǎi pop gan

## likes & dislikes

I thought it was ...    ຂ້ອຍໄດ້ຄິດວ່າ     kòy dǎi kit wah
      ມັນ ...     mán ...
It's ...    ມັນ ...     mán ...
   awful    ຂີ້ຮ້າຍ     kêe lâi
   great    ຖືກ     kák
   interesting    ເປັນຕາສົນໃຈ     ɓen ɗah sŏn jai

Do you like ...?    ເຈົ້າມັກ ... ບໍ່?     jôw mak ... bor
I (don't) like ...    ຂ້ອຍ (ບໍ່) ມັກ ...     kóy (bor) mak ...
   art    ສິລະປະ     sí-la-ɓà
   sport    ກິລາ     gi-láh

## eating & drinking

I'd like ..., please.    ... ຂ້ອຍຢາກໄດ້     ... kòy yahk dǎi
   the nonsmoking    ບ່ອນປອດຢາສູບ     born ɓort yah sòop
   section
   the smoking    ບ່ອນສູບຢາໄດ້     born sòop yah dǎi
   section
   a table for (four)    ໂຕະສຳລັບ     ɗôh săm-làp
      (ສີ່) ຄົນ     (see) kón

**Lao**

**I don't want any meat.**
ຂ້ອຍບໍ່ເອົາຊີ້ນສັດ

kòy bor ow sêen sát

**What would you recommend?**
ມີຫຍັງພິເສດບໍ່?

mée nyang pi-sét bor

## Would you like a drink?
ເຈົ້າຢາກດື່ມນ້ຳບໍ່?
jôw yáhk deum nâm bor

| | | |
|---|---|---|
| I'll have a ... | ຂ້ອຍຂໍ ... | kòy kŏr ... |
| Cheers! | ເຊີນດື່ມ | séun deum |
| | | |
| I'd like (the) ... | ຂໍ ... ແດ່ | kŏr ... dàa |
| bill | ເຊັກ | sék |
| menu | ລາຍການອາຫານ | lái gahn ah-hähn |
| that dish | ຈານນັ້ນ | jahn nàn |
| | | |
| coffee/tea | ກາເຟ/ຊາ | gah-fáir/sáh |
| (mineral) water | ນ້ຳ (ແຮ່ຫາດ) | nâm (háa tâht) |
| glass of (wine) | (ວາຍ) ຈອກໜຶ່ງ | (wai) jork neung |
| bottle of (beer) | (ເບຍ) ແກ້ວໜຶ່ງ | (bee-a) gâa-ou neung |
| | | |
| breakfast | ອາຫານເຊົ້າ | ah-hähn sôw |
| lunch | ອາຫານທ່ຽງ | ah-hähn tee-ang |
| dinner | ອາຫານແລງ | ah-hähn láang |

## exploring

| | | |
|---|---|---|
| Where's the ...? | ... ຢູ່ໃສ? | ... yoo sãi |
| bank | ທະນາຄານ | ta-náh-káhn |
| hotel | ໂຮງແຮມ | hóhng háam |
| post office | ຫ້ອງການໄປສະນີ | hòrng gahn bai-sá-ni |
| | | |
| Where are the ...? | ... ຢູ່ໃສ? | ... yoo sãi |
| bars | ບາ | bah |
| clubs | ສະໂມສອນ | sà-móh-sörn |
| restaurants | ຮ້ານອາຫານ | hâhn ah-hähn |

78

**Can you show me (on the map)?**
ເຈົ້າບອກທາງຂ້ອຍ
(ຢູ່ໃນແຜນທີ່) ໄດ້ບໍ່?
jôw bork táhng kòy
(yoo nai păan tee) dâi bor

**What time does it open/close?**
ມັນເປີດ/ປິດເວລາຈັກໂມງ?
man beut/bìt wáir-láh ják móhng

**Is there an admission charge?**
ເກັບຄ່າຜ່ານປະຕູບໍ່?
gép káh pahn bà-đoo bor

**When's the next tour?**
ທ່ອງທ່ຽວເທື່ອຕໍ່ໄປແມ່ນ
ເວລາໃດ?
tòrng têe-o teu-a đór bai maan
wáir-láh dai

**Where can I buy a ticket?**
ຂ້ອຍຊື້ປີ້ຢູ່ໃສ?
kòy sêu bêe yoo săi

| | | |
|---|---|---|
| **My luggage has been ...** | ກະເປົາເຄື່ອງນຸ່ງ ຂອງຂ້ອຍ ... | ga-bow keu·ang noong körng kòy ... |
| lost | ເສຍ | sée-a |
| stolen | ຖຶກລັກ | teuk lák |
| **One ... ticket to (Khammuan), please.** | ປີ້ ... ໜຶ່ງໄປ (ຄໍ່ມ່ວນ) ແຕ່ | bêe ... neung bai (kàm-muan) dáa |
| one-way | ປີ້ຖ້ຽວດຽວ | bêe têe-o dèe-o |
| return | ປີ້ໄປກັບ | bêe bài gáp |
| **Is this the ... to (Luang Nam Tha)?** | ນີ້ແມ່ນໄປ ... (ຫຼວງນ້ຳທາ) ບໍ່? | nêe maan bai ... (lŏo·ang nâm tâh) bor |
| boat | ເຮືອ | héu·a |
| bus | ລົດເມ | lot máir |
| plane | ເຮືອບິນ | héu·a bin |
| **What time's the ... bus?** | ຈັກໂມງ ລົດເມ ... ອອກ? | ják móhng lot máir ... ork |
| first | ຄັນທີ່ໜຶ່ງ | kán tee neung |
| last | ຄັນສຸດທ້າຍ | kán sút tâi |
| **I'd like a taxi ...** | ຂ້ອຍຍາກຂີ່ລົດ ແທກຊີ່ອອກ ... | kòy yahk kee lót táak-sée ork ... |
| at (9am) | ເວລາ (ເກົ້າ ໂມງເຊົ້າ) | wáir-láh (gòw móhng sôw) |
| tomorrow | ມື້ອື່ນ | mêu eun |

**How much is it to (Vientiane)?**

ໄປ (ວຽງຈັນ) ເທົ່າໃດ?   bài (wée-ang-jan) tow dai

**Please put the meter on.**

ກະລຸນາເປີດມີເຕີ້ແດ່   gá-lu-náh béut mi-đêu dáa

**Please take me to (this address).**

ກະລຸນາພາຂ້ອຍໄປ
(ທີ່ຢູ່ນີ້) ແດ່   gá-lu-náh páh kòy bài
(tee yoo nêe) dáa

**Please stop here.**

ກະລຸນາຈອດຢູ່ນີ້   gá-lu-náh jort yoo nêe

# shopping

**Where's the (market)?**

(ຕະຫລາດ)ຢູ່ໃສ?   (đa-làht) yoo säi

**How much is it?**

ລາຄາເທົ່າໃດ?   láh-káh tow dai

**Can you write down the price?**

ເຈົ້າຽູນລາຄາໃສ່ໄດ້ບໍ?   jôw kêe-an láh-káh sai dâi bor

**That's too expensive.**

ຂ້ອຍຄິດວ່າແພງໂພດ   kòy kít wah páang pôht

**There's a mistake in the bill.**

ບິນຽຽນບໍ່ຖືກ   bín kêe-an bor tèuk

**The quality isn't very good.**

ຄຸນມະພາບບໍ່ດີປານໃດ   kún-na-pàhp boh dée bahn dai

| | | |
|---|---|---|
| **I'd like ..., please.** | ຂ້ອຍຂໍ ... ແດ່ | kòy kör ... dàa |
| a refund | ເອົາເງິນຄືນ | ow ngeun kéun |
| to return this | ສົ່ງເຄື່ອງນີ້ຄືນ | sòng keu-ang nêe ké |
| **I'd like ..., please.** | ເອົາ ... ໃຫ້ຂ້ອຍແດ່ | ow ... hâi kòy dàa |
| my change | ເງິນທອນຂອງ | ngéun torn körng |
| | ຂ້ອຍ | kòy |
| a receipt | ໃບຮັບເງິນ | bai hap ngéun |
| **Do you accept ...?** | ເຈົ້າເອົາ ... ບໍ? | jôw ow ... bor |
| credit cards | ບັດເຄຣດິດ | bát klàir-dít |
| travellers cheques | ເຊັກທ່ອງທ່ຽວ | sék torng têe-o |

# working

| English | Lao | Transliteration |
|---|---|---|
| I'm attending a … | ຂ້ອຍເຂົ້າຮ່ວມ … | kòy kòw hôo-am … |
| conference | ກອງປະຊຸມໃຫຍ່ | gorng bá-súm nyai |
| course | ການຝຶກອົບຮົມ | gahn feuk óp-hóm |
| meeting | ການປະຊຸມ | gahn bá-súm |
| trade fair | ຕະຫຼາດນັດ | đá-láhd-nad |
| | ການຄ້າ | gahn-kâh |
| I'm here for … | ຂ້ອຍມາພີ້ສຳລັບ … | kòy máh pêe săm-lap … |
| (two) days | (ສອງ) ມື້ | (sŏrng) méu |
| (three) weeks | (ສາມ) ອາທິດ | (săhm) ah-tit |
| I'm with … | ຂ້ອຍມາກັບ … | kòy máh gáp … |
| my colleagues | ເພື່ອນຮ່ວມງານ | péu-an hoo-am ngáhn |
| | ຂອງຂ້ອຍ | kŏrng kòy |
| (two) others | ອີກ (ສອງ) ຄົນ | èek (sŏrng) kón |

I'm alone.
ຂ້ອຍມາຜູ້ດຽວ    kòy máh pòo dèe-oh

I have an appointment with …
ຂ້ອຍມີນັດກັບ …    kòy mêe nad gáp …

I'm staying at the (Lane Xang Hotel), room (304).

| | |
|---|---|
| ຂ້ອຍພັກຢູ່ | kòy pák yoo |
| (ໂຮງແຮມລ້ານຊ້າງ) | (hóhng háam lâhn sâhng) |
| ຫ້ອງ (ສາມສູນສີ່) | hòrng (săhm sŏon see) |

| English | Lao | Transliteration |
|---|---|---|
| Where's the …? | … ຢູ່ໃສ? | … yoo săi |
| business centre | ສູນທຸລະກິດ | sŏon tu-la-gít |
| conference | ການປະຊຸມໃຫຍ່ | gahn bá-súm nyai |
| meeting | ການປະຊຸມ | gahn bá-súm |
| I need … | ຂ້ອຍຕ້ອງການ … | kòy đôrng gahn … |
| a computer | ຄອມພິວເຕີ | kórm-pew-đeu |
| an internet connection | ຕໍ່ອິນເຕີເນດ | đor in-đeu-náirt |
| an interpreter | ຄົນແປພາສາ | kón baa páh-săh |
| to send a fax | ສົ່ງແຟກ | song fâak |

81

Lao

| Here's my ... | ອັ້ນແມ່ນ ... ຂອງຂ້ອຍ | an nêe máan ... kõrng |
| business card | ນາມບັດ | náhm bát |
| fax number | ເບີແຟກ | bèu fâak |
| work number | ເບີທ້ອງການ | bèu hòrng gahn |

**Can I have your business card?**
ຂໍນາມບັດຂອງທ່ານໄດ້ບໍ?
kõr náhm bát kõrng tâhn dâi bor

**That went very well.**
ອັນນນໄປໄດ້ໂດຍດີ
an nân bai dâi doy dee

**Thank you for your time.**
ຂໍຂອບໃຈທ່ານທີ່ໄດ້ສະລະ
ເວລາ
kõr kòrp jai tâhn tée dâi sá-la wáir-láh

**Shall we go for a drink?**
ໄປດື່ມນ້ຳບໍ
bai deum nâm bor

**Shall we go for a meal?**
ໄປກິນເຂົ້າບໍ
bai gin kòw bor

**It's on me.**
ຂ້ອຍລ້ຽງ
kòy lêe·ang

## emergencies

| Help! | ຊ່ວຍແດ່ | soo·ay daa |
| Stop! | ຢຸດ | yút |
| Go away! | ໜີໄປ | nêe bai |
| Thief! | ຄົນຂີ້ລັກ | kón kêe lak |
| Fire! | ໄຟໃໝ້ | fái mâi |

| Call ...! | ຊ່ວຍເອີ້ນ ... ແດ່ | soo·ay êun ... hâi dàa |
| an ambulance | ລົດໂຮງໝໍ | lot hóhng mõr |
| a doctor | ທ່ານໝໍໃຫ້ | tahn mõr |
| the police | ຕຳຫລວດ | đam-luat |

**Could you help me, please?**
ເຈົ້າຊ່ວຍຂ້ອຍໄດ້ບໍ?
jôw soo·ay kòy dâi bor

**I'm lost.**
ຂ້ອຍຫລົງທາງ
kòy lõng táhng

**Where are the toilets?**
ຫ້ອງນ້ຳຢູ່ໃສ?
hòrng nâm yoo sãi

82

# Mandarin

China isn't a country – it's a different world. Be prepared to cross the border.

# Pronunciation

| Vowels | | Consonants | |
|---|---|---|---|
| **Symbol** | **English sound** | **Symbol** | **English sound** |
| a (an/ang) | father (fun, sung) | b | bed |
| ai | aisle | c | hats |
| ao | now | ch | cheat |
| e (en/eng) | her (broken, Deng) | d | dog |
| ei | pay | f | fat |
| i (in/ing) | peel (pin, ping) | g | go |
| i (after c/s/z) | girl | h | hat |
| | | j | joke |
| i (after ch/sh/zh/r) | like the 'r' in Grrr! | k | kit |
| | | l | lot |
| ia | yard | m | man |
| ian | yen | n | not |
| iang | young | ng | ring |
| iao | yowl | p | pet |
| ie | yes | q | cheat |
| iong | Jung | r | red |
| iu | yolk | s | sun |
| o (ong) | more (Jung) | sh | shot |
| ou | low | t | top |
| u (un) | tool (tune) | w | win |
| ua | wah! | x | shot |
| uai | why | y | yes |
| uan | won | z | sounds |
| uan (after j/q/x/y) | went | zh | gem |
| uang | swung | | |
| ue | you wet | |
| ui | way | |
| uo | war | |
| ü (and u after q/j/x) | 'new' pronounced with rounded lips | |

In this chapter, we've used Pinyin (the official system of writing Chinese using the Roman alphabet) in our pronunciation guides.

For **tones**, see page 12.

Mandarin

84

# essentials

| | | |
|---|---|---|
| Yes. | 是。 | Shì. |
| No. | 不是。 | Bùshì. |
| Hello. (general) | 你好。 | Nǐhǎo. |
| Hello. (Beijing) | 您好。 | Nínhǎo. |
| Goodbye. | 再见。 | Zàijiàn. |
| Please ... | 请…… | Qǐng ... |
| Thank you (very much). | (非常) 谢谢你。 | (Fēicháng) Xièxie nǐ. |
| You're welcome. | 不客气。 | Bù kèqi. |
| Excuse me. | 劳驾。 | Láojià. |
| Sorry. | 对不起。 | Duìbùqǐ. |
| Do you speak English? | 你会说英文吗？ | Nǐ huìshuō Yīngwén ma? |
| Do you understand? | 你明白吗？ | Nǐ míngbai ma? |
| I (don't) understand. | 我 (不) 明白。 | Wǒ (bù) míngbai. |

# chatting

## introductions

| | | |
|---|---|---|
| Mr | 先生 | xiānsheng |
| Mrs/Ms | 女士/小姐 | nǚshì/xiǎojiě |

**How are you? (general)**
你好吗？                              Nǐhǎo ma?

**How are you? (Beijing)**
您好吗？                              Nínhǎo ma?

**Fine. And you?**
好。你呢？                            Hǎo. Nǐ ne?

**What's your name?**
你叫什么名字？                        Nǐ jiào shénme míngzi?

**My name is ...**
我叫……                               Wǒ jiào ...

**I'm pleased to meet you.**
幸会。                                Xìnghuì.

| Here's my ... | 给你我的…… | Gěinǐ wǒde ... |
| What's your ...? | 你的……是什么？ | Nǐde ... shì shénme? |
| address | 地址 | dìzhǐ |
| email address | 邮箱地址 | yóuxiāng dìzhǐ |
| phone number | 电话号码 | diànhuà hàomǎ |

| What's your occupation? | 你做什么工作？ | Nǐ zuò shénme gōngzuò? |
| I'm a ... | 我是…… | Wǒ shì ... |
| businessperson | 商人 | shāngrén |
| student | 学生 | xuésheng |

| Where are you from? | | |
| 你从哪儿来？ | | Nǐ cóngnǎr lái? |
| I'm from (England). | | |
| 我从（英国）来。 | | Wǒ cóng (Yīngguó) lái. |
| Are you married? | | |
| 你结婚了吗？ | | Nǐ jiéhūn le ma? |

| I'm ... | 我…… | Wǒ ... |
| married | 结婚 | jiéhūn |
| single | 单身 | dānshēn |

| How old are you? | | |
| 你多大了？ | | Nǐ duōdà le? |
| I'm ... years old. | | |
| 我……岁。 | | Wǒ ... suì. |

## making conversation

| What's the weather like? | | |
| 天气怎么样？ | | Tiānqì zěnmeyàng? |

| It's ... | 天气…… | Tiānqì ... |
| cold | 冷 | lěng |
| hot | 热 | rè |
| raining | 下雨 | xiàyǔ |
| snowing | 下雪 | xiàxuě |

**Do you live here?**
你住这里吗？　　　　Nǐ zhù zhèlǐ ma?

**What are you doing?**
你在干吗？　　　　　Nǐ zài gànma?

## meeting up

**What time will we meet?**
几点钟碰头？　　　　Jǐdiǎnzhōng pèngtóu?

**Where will we meet?**
在哪里碰头？　　　　Zài nǎli pèngtóu?

**Let's meet at ...**　　我们在……　　　Wǒmen zài ...
　　　　　　　　　　见面。　　　　　jiànmiàn.
　　**(eight) o'clock**　（八）点钟　　（bā)diǎn zhōng
　　**the entrance**　　门口　　　　　ménkǒu

**It's been great meeting you.**
认识你实在很高兴。　　Rènshi nǐ shízài hěn gāoxìng.

# I love it here!
# 我很喜欢这里！
## Wǒ hěn xǐhuān zhèlǐ!

## likes & dislikes

**I thought it was ...**　我觉得……　　Wǒ juéde ...
**It's ...**　　　　　　它……　　　Tā ...
　　**awful**　　　　　很差劲　　　hěn chàjìn
　　**great**　　　　　很棒　　　　hěn bàng
　　**interesting**　　很有意思　　hěn yǒu yìsi

**Do you like ...?**　　你喜欢……吗？　Nǐ xǐhuān ... ma?
**I (don't) like ...**　我（不）　　　Wǒ (bù)
　　　　　　　　　　喜欢……　　　xǐhuān ...

　　**art**　　　　　　艺术　　　　yìshù
　　**sport**　　　　　体育　　　　tǐyù

Mandarin

# eating & drinking

Mandarin

| I'd like ..., please. | 我要…… | Wǒ yào ... |
|---|---|---|
| the nonsmoking section | 不吸烟的桌子 | bùxīyān de zhuōzi |
| the smoking section | 吸烟的桌子 | xīyān de zhuōzi |
| a table for (five) | 一张（五个人的）桌子 | yìzhāng (wǔge rén)de zhuōzi |

**Do you have vegetarian food?**
有没有素食食品？　Yǒuméiyǒu sùshí shípín?

**What would you recommend?**
有什么菜可以推荐的？　Yǒu shénme cài kěyǐ tuījiàn de?

## Would you like a drink?
## 你想喝点什么？
### Nǐ xiǎng hēdiǎn shénme?

| I'll have a ... | 我来一个…… | Wǒ lái yìge ... |
|---|---|---|
| Cheers! | 干杯！ | Gānbēi! |
| I'd like the ..., please. | 请拿来…… | Qǐng ná lái ... |
| drink list | 酒水单 | jiǔshuǐ dān |
| menu | 菜单 | càidān |
| I'll have that. | 来一个吧。 | Lái yìge ba. |
| The bill, please! | 买单！ | Mǎidān! |
| (cup of) coffee/tea | （一杯）咖啡/茶 | (yìbēi) kāfēi/chá |
| (mineral) water | （矿泉）水 | (kuàngquán) shuǐ |
| glass of (wine) | 一杯（葡萄酒） | yìbēi (pútáo jiǔ) |
| bottle of (beer) | 一瓶（啤酒） | yìpíng (píjiǔ) |
| breakfast | 早饭 | zǎofàn |
| lunch | 午饭 | wǔfàn |
| dinner | 晚饭 | wǎnfàn |

# exploring

| Where's the ...? | ······在哪儿? | ... zài nǎr? |
|---|---|---|
| bank | 银行 | Yínháng |
| hotel | 酒店 | Jiǔdiàn |
| post office | 邮局 | Yóujú |

| Where can I find ...? | ······怎么找? | ... zěnme zhǎo? |
|---|---|---|
| bars | 酒吧 | Jiǔbā |
| clubs | 夜总会 | Yèzǒnghuì |
| restaurants | 饭馆 | Fànguǎn |

**Can you show me where it is on the map?**
请帮我在地图上找。 Qǐng bāngwǒ zài dìtú shàng zhǎo.

**What time does it open/close?**
几点开门/关门? Jǐdiǎn kāimén/guānmén?

**What's the admission charge?**
门票多少钱? Ménpiào duōshǎo qián?

**When's the next tour?**
下一个向导游是
什么时候? Xiàyīge xiàngdǎoyóu shì shénme shíhòu?

**Where can I buy a ticket?**
哪里买票? Nǎli mǎipiào?

| One ... ticket to (Dalian), please. | 一张到(大连)的······票。 | Yìzhāng dào (Dàlián) de ... piào. |
|---|---|---|
| one-way | 单程 | dānchéng |
| return | 双程 | shuāngchéng |

| My luggage has been ... | 我的行李被······了。 | Wǒde xíngli bèi ... le. |
|---|---|---|
| lost | 丢 | diū |
| stolen | 偷走 | tōuzǒu |

| Is this the ... to (Hangzhou)? | 这个······到(杭州)去吗? | Zhège ... dào (Hángzhōu) qù ma? |
|---|---|---|
| bus | 车 | chē |
| plane | 飞机 | fēijī |
| train | 火车 | huǒchē |

Mandarin

| What time's the ... bus? | ……车 几点走？ | ... chē jǐdiǎn zǒu? |
|---|---|---|
| first | 首趟 | Shǒutàng |
| last | 末趟 | Mòtàng |
| next | 下一趟 | Xià yītàng |
| I'd like a taxi ... | 我要订一辆 出租车，…… | Wǒ yào dìng yīliàng chūzū chē ... |
| at (9am) | （早上9 点钟）出发 | (zǎoshàng jiǔ diǎn zhōng) chūfā |
| tomorrow | 明天 | míngtiān |

**How much is it to (the Great Wall)?**
到(长城)多少钱？ Dào (Chángchéng) duōshǎo qián?

**Please put the meter on.**
请打表。 Qǐng dǎbiǎo.

**Please take me to (this address).**
请带我到(这个地址)。 Qǐng dàiwǒ dào (zhège dìzhǐ).

**Please stop here.**
请在这儿停。 Qǐng zài zhèr tíng.

# shopping

| Where's the market? | 菜市场在哪儿？ | Càishìchǎng zài nǎr? |
|---|---|---|
| How much is it? | 多少钱？ | Duōshǎo qián? |
| Can you write down the price? | 请把价钱 写下来。 | Qǐng bǎ jiàqián xiěxià lái. |
| That's too expensive. | 太贵了。 | Tàiguì le. |
| There's a mistake in the bill. | 帐单上有问题。 | Zhàngdān shàng yǒu wè |
| It's faulty. | 有毛病。 | Yǒu máobìng. |
| Could I have a receipt, please? | 请给我开发票。 | Qǐng gěiwǒ kāi fāpiào. |
| I'd like ..., please. | 可以……吗？ | Kěyǐ ... ma? |
| my change | 找零钱 | zhǎo língqián |
| a refund | 退钱 | tuìqián |
| to return this | 退换这个 | tuìhuàn zhège |

| Do you accept ...? | 你们收……吗? | Nǐmen shōu ... ma? |
| credit cards | 信用卡 | xìnyòng kǎ |
| travellers cheques | 旅行支票 | lǚxíng zhīpiào |

# working

| I'm attending a ... | 我来参加一个…… | Wǒ lái cānjiā yīge ... |
| conference | 研讨会 | yántǎohuì |
| course | 培训班 | péixùnbān |
| meeting | 会议 | huìyì |
| trade fair | 洽谈会 | qiàtánhuì |

| I'm here for ... | 我要呆…… | Wǒ yào dāi ... |
| (two) days | (两)天 | (liǎng) tiān |
| (three) weeks | (三)个星期 | (sān) ge xīngqī |

| I'm with ... | 我跟……一块来的。 | Wǒ gēn ... yīkuàilái de. |
| my colleague(s) | (几个)同事 | (jǐge) tóngshì |
| (two) others | (两个)人 | (liǎngge) rén |

I'm alone.
我一个人来的。　　　　Wǒ yīgérén lái de.

I have an appointment with ...
我跟……有约。　　　　Wǒ gēn ... yǒuyuē.

I'm staying at the ..., room ...
我住在……，　　　　Wǒ zhù zài ...,
……号房间。　　　　... hào fángjiān.

| Where's the ...? | ……在哪儿? | ... zài nǎr? |
| business centre | 商务中心 | Shāngwù zhōngxīn |
| conference | 研讨会 | Yántǎohuì |
| meeting | 会议 | Huìyì |

| I need ... | 我需要…… | Wǒ xūyào ... |
| a computer | 一台电脑 | yītái diànnǎo |
| an internet connection | 上网 | shàngwǎng |
| an interpreter | 一位翻译 | yīwèi fānyì |
| to send a fax | 发一个传真 | fā yīge chuánzhēn |

Mandarin

| Here's my ... | 给你的…… | Gěinǐ wǒde ... |
|---|---|---|
| business card | 名片 | míngpiàn |
| fax number | 传真号码 | chuánzhēn hàomǎ |
| mobile number | 手机号码 | shǒujī hàomǎ |
| pager number | 寻呼号码 | xúnhū hàomǎ |
| work number | 公司电话 | gōngsī diànhuà |

**Can I have your business card?**
你有名片吗？
nǐ yǒu míngpiàn ma?

**That went very well.**
刚才开得很好。
Gāngcái kāide hěnhǎo.

**Thank you for your time.**
谢谢你们的关照。
Xièxie nǐmende guānzhào.

**Shall we go for a drink/meal?**
咱们是不是
出去喝杯酒/吃饭？
Zánmen shìbùshì
chūqu hēbēijiǔ/chīfàn?

**It's on me.**
我请客。
Wǒ qǐng kè.

# emergencies

| Help! | 救命！ | Jiùmìng! |
|---|---|---|
| Stop! | 站住！ | Zhànzhu! |
| Go away! | 走开！ | Zǒukāi! |
| Thief! | 小偷！ | Xiǎotōu! |
| Fire! | 着火啦！ | Zháohuǒ la! |

**Call an ambulance!**
请叫一辆急救车！
Qǐng jiào yīliàng jíjiù chē!

**Call a doctor!**
请叫医生过来！
Qǐng jiào yīshēng guòlái!

**Please telephone 110.**
请打110。
Qǐng dǎ yāo yāo líng.

**Could you help me, please?**
你能帮我吗？
Nǐ néng bāngwǒ ma?

**I'm lost.**
我迷路了。
Wǒ mí lù le.

**Where are the toilets?**
厕所在哪儿？
Cèsuǒ zài nǎr?

# Thai

Thailand – the land of sun, *tom yum* and spiritual enlightenment.

# Pronunciation

| Vowels | | Consonants | |
|---|---|---|---|
| **Symbol** | **English sound** | **Symbol** | **English sound** |
| a | run | b | bed |
| aa | act | ฿ | spin |
| aa·ou | aa followed by u | ch | cheat |
| ah | father | d | dog |
| ai | aisle (longer) | đ | stop |
| air | fair | f | fat |
| e | bed | g | go |
| ee | see | h | hat |
| eu | nurse | j | joke |
| ew | ee pronounced with rounded lips | k | kit |
| | | l | lot |
| i | hit | m | man |
| o | pot | n | not |
| oh | note | ng | ring |
| oo | zoo | p | pet |
| or | for | r | red |
| ow | how | s | sun |
| oy | toy | t | top |
| u | put | w | win |
| | | y | yes |

In this chapter, we've used hyphens to separate syllables in a word (eg ang-grit), and further divided separate vowel sounds within the one syllable with a dot (eg kĕe·an).
The ฿ sound is halfway between a 'b' and a 'p', and the đ sound is halfway between a 'd' and a 't'.
For **tones**, see page 12.

# essentials

| | | |
|---|---|---|
| Yes./No. | ใช่/ไม่ | châi/mâi |
| Hello. | สวัสดี | sà-wàt-dee |
| Goodbye. | ลาก่อน | lah gòrn |
| Please. | ขอ | kŏr |
| Thank you | ขอบคุณ | kòrp kun |
| (very much). | (มากๆ) | (mâhk mâhk) |
| You're welcome. | ยินดี | yin dee |
| Excuse me./Sorry. | ขอโทษ | kŏr tôht |

**Do you speak English?**
พูดภาษาอังกฤษได้ไหม · pôot pah-săh ang-grìt dâi măi

**Do you understand?**
คุณเข้าใจไหม · kun kôw jai măi

**I (don't) understand.**
ผม/ดิฉัน (ไม่) เข้าใจ · pŏm/dì-chăn (mâi) kôw jai m/f

# chatting

## introductions

| | | |
|---|---|---|
| Mr | นาย | nai |
| Mrs | นาง | nahng |
| Miss | นางสาว | nahng sŏw |

**How are you?**
สบายดีไหม · sà-bai dee măi

**Fine. And you?**
สบายดีครับ/ค่ะ · sà-bai dee kráp/kâ
แล้วคุณล่ะ · láa·ou kun lâ m/f

**What's your name?**
คุณชื่ออะไร · kun chêu à-rai

**My name is ...**
ผม/ดิฉันชื่อ ... · pŏm/dì-chăn chêu ... m/f

**I'm pleased to meet you.**
ยินดีที่ได้รู้จัก · yin-dee têe dâi róo jàk

Thai

| Here's my ... | นี่คือ ... ของ | nêe keu ... kŏrng |
| | ผม/ดิฉัน | pŏm/dì-chăn m/f |
| What's your ...? | ... ของคุณ | ... kŏrng kun |
| | คืออะไร | keu à-ra |
| (email) address | ที่อยู่ (อีเมล) | têe yòo (ee-men) |
| phone number | เบอร์ | beu |
| What's your occupation? | คุณมีอาชีพอะไร | kun mee ah-chêep à-rai |
| I'm a/an ... | ฉันเป็น ... | chăn ben ... |
| office worker | พนักงาน | pá-nák ngahn |
| | สำนักงาน | săm-nák ngahn |
| student | นักศึกษา | nák sèuk-săh |

**Where are you from?**
คุณมาจากไหน                        kun mah jàhk năi

**I'm from (England).**
ผม/ดิฉันมาจาก                      pŏm/dì-chăn mah
ประเทศ (อังกฤษ)                    jàhk brà-têt (ang-grìt) m/f

**Are you married?**
คุณแต่งงานหรือยัง                   kun đàang ngahn rĕu yang

| I'm ... | ผม/ดิฉัน ... | pŏm/dì-chăn ... m/f |
| married | แต่งงานแล้ว | đàang ngahn láa-ou |
| single | เป็นโสดอยู่ | ben sòht yòo |

**How old are you?**
คุณอายุเท่าไร                         kun ah-yú tôw-rai

**I'm ... years old.**
ฉันอายุ ... ปี                        chăn ah-yú ... bee

## making conversation

**What's the weather like?**
อากาศเป็นอย่างไร                    ah-gàht ben yàhng rai

| It's ... | มัน ... | man ... |
| cold | หนาว | nŏw |
| (very) hot | ร้อน (มาก) | rórn (mâhk) |
| rainy | มีฝน | mee fŏn |
| windy | มีลม | mee lom |

**Do you live here?**
คุณอยู่ที่นี่หรือเปล่า — kun yòo têe née rĕu blòw

**What are you doing?**
กำลังทำอะไรอยู่ — gam-lang tam à-rai yòo

## meeting up

**What time will we meet?**
จะพบกันกี่โมง — jà póp gan gèe mohng

**Where will we meet?**
จะพบกันที่ไหน — jà póp gan têe năi

| Let's meet at ... | พบกัน ... ดีไหม | póp gan ... dee măi |
|---|---|---|
| (8pm) | (สองทุ่ม) | (sŏng tûm) |
| the entrance | ที่ ทางเข้า | têe tahng kôw |

**It's been great meeting you.**
ดีใจมากที่ได้พบกับคุณ — dee jai mâhk têe dâi póp gàp kun

# I love it here!
ชอบที่นี่มาก
chôrp têe née mâhk

## likes & dislikes

| I thought it | ผม/ดิฉัน | pŏm/dì-chăn |
|---|---|---|
| was ... | คิดว่ามัน ... | kít wâh man ... m/f |
| It's ... | มัน ... | man ... |
| awful | สุดแย่ | sùt yâa |
| great | เยี่ยม | yêe-am |
| interesting | น่าสนใจ | nâh sŏn-jai |

| Do you like ...? | ชอบ ... ไหม | chôrp ... măi |
|---|---|---|
| I (don't) like ... | ผม/ดิฉัน | pŏm/dì-chăn |
| | (ไม่) ชอบ ... | (mâi) chôrp ... m/f |
| art | ศิลปะ | sĭn-lá-bà |
| sport | กีฬา | gee-lah |

97

# eating & drinking

I'd like ..., please. ขอ ... หน่อย kŏr ... nòy
   the nonsmoking ที่เขตห้ามสูบ têe kèt hâhm sòop
   section บุหรี่ bù-rèe
   the smoking ที่เขตสูบบุหรี่ têe kèt sòop bù-rèe
   section ได้ dâi
   a table for (five) โต๊ะสำหรับ dó săm-ràp
    (ห้า) คน (hâh) kon

**Do you have vegetarian food?**
มีอาหารเจไหม mee ah-hăhn jair măi

**What would you recommend?**
คุณแนะนำอะไรบ้าง kun náa-nam à-rai bâhng

**I'll have that.**
เอาอันนั้นนะ ow an nán ná

## Would you like a drink?
### จะดื่มอะไรไหม
### jà dèum à-rai măi

I'd like the ..., ขอ ... หน่อย kŏr ... nòy
please.
   bill ปิลล์ bin
   drink list รายการเครื่อง rai gahn krêu-ang
    ดื่ม dèum
   menu รายการอาหาร rai gahn ah-hăhn

(cup of ) coffee/tea กาแฟ/ชา gah-faa/chah
    (ถ้วยหนึ่ง ) (tôo-ay nèung)
(mineral) water น้ำ (แร่อัดลม) nám (râa àt lom)
glass of (wine) (ไวน์) แก้วหนึ่ง (wai) gâa-ou nèung
bottle of (beer) (เบียร์) ขวดหนึ่ง (bee-a) kòo-at nèung

breakfast อาหารเช้า ah-hăhn chów
lunch อาหารกลางวัน ah-hăhn glahng wan
dinner อาหารเย็น ah-hăhn yen

# exploring

| **Where's the ...?** | ... อยู่ที่ไหน | ... yòo têe năi |
|---|---|---|
| bank | ธนาคาร | tá-nah-kahn |
| hotel | โรงแรม | rohng raam |
| post office | ที่ทำการ | têe tam gahn |
| | ไปรษณีย์ | brai-sà-nee |

| **Where are the ...?** | ... อยู่ที่ไหน | ... yòo têe năi |
|---|---|---|
| clubs | ไนท์คลับ | nai kláp |
| pubs | ผับ | pàp |
| restaurants | ที่ทานอาหาร | têe tahn ah-hǎhn |

**Can you show me (on the map)?**
ให้ดู (ในแผนที่) ได้ไหม   hâi doo (nai pǎan têe) dâi mǎi

**What time does it open/close?**
เปิด/ปิดกี่โมง   bèut/bìt gèe mohng

**What's the admission charge?**
ค่าเข้าเท่าไร   kâh kôw tôw-rai

**When's the next tour?**
ทัวร์ต่อไปออกกี่โมง   too-a dòr bai òrk gèe mohng

**Where can I buy a ticket?**
ต้องซื้อตั๋วที่ไหน   đôrng séu đŏo-a têe năi

| **One ... ticket to** | ขอตั๋ว ... ไป | kŏr đŏo-a ... bai |
|---|---|---|
| **(Chiang Mai), please.** | (เชียงใหม่) | (chee-ang mài) |
| one-way | เที่ยวเดียว | têe-o dee-o |
| return | ไปกลับ | bai glàp |

| **My luggage** | กระเป๋าของผม/ | grà-bŏw kŏrng pŏm/ |
|---|---|---|
| **has been ...** | ดิฉันโดน ... แล้ว | dì-chǎn dohn ... láa-ou m/f |
| lost | หายไป | hǎi bai |
| stolen | ขโมย | kà-moy |

| **Is this the ... to** | อันนี้เป็น ... ไป | an née ben ... bai |
|---|---|---|
| **(Chiang Mai)?** | (เชียงใหม่) | (chee-ang mài) |
| | ใช่ไหม | châi mǎi |
| bus | รถเมล์ | rót mair |
| plane | เครื่องบิน | krêu-ang bin |
| train | รถไฟ | rót fai |

| When's the ... bus? | รถเมล์คัน ... มาเมื่อไร | rót mair kan ... mah mêu·a rai |
|---|---|---|
| first | แรก | râak |
| last | สุดท้าย | sùt tái |
| next | ต่อไป | đòr bai |

| I'd like a taxi ... | ต้องการรถ แท็กซี่ ... | đôrng gahn rót táak-sêe ... |
|---|---|---|
| at (9am) | เมื่อ (สามโมงเช้า) | mêu·a (sǎhm mohng chów) |
| tomorrow | พรุ่งนี้ | prûng née |

**How much is it to ...?**
ไป ... เท่าไร · pai ... tôw-rai

**Please put the meter on.**
ขอเปิดมิเตอร์ด้วย · kŏr bèut mí-đeu dôo·ay

**Please take me to (this address).**
ขอพาไป (ที่นี่) · kŏr pah bai (têe née)

**Please stop here.**
ขอหยุดตรงนี้ · kŏr yùt đrong née

# shopping

| Where's the (market)? | (ตลาด) อยู่ที่ไหน | (đà-làht) yòo têe nǎi |
|---|---|---|
| How much is it? | เท่าไรครับ/คะ | tôw-rai kráp/ká m/f |
| Can you write down the price? | เขียนราคาให้ หน่อยได้ไหม | kěe·an rah-kah hâi nòy dâi mǎi |
| That's too expensive. | แพงไป | paang bai |
| There's a mistake in the bill. | บิลใบนี้ผิดนะ ครับ/ค่ะ | bin bai née pìt ná kráp/kâ m/f |
| It's faulty. | มันบกพร่อง | man bòk prôrng |

| I'd like ..., please. | อยากจะ... ครับ/ค่ะ | yàhk jà ... kráp/kâ m/f |
|---|---|---|
| a refund | ได้เงินคืน | dâi ngeun keun |
| to return this | เอามาคืน | ow mah keun |

| I'd like ..., please. | ขอ ... หน่อย | kŏr ... nòy |
|---|---|---|
| my change | เงินทอน | ngeun torn |
| a receipt | ใบเสร็จ | bai sèt |

| Do you accept ...? | รับ ... ไหม | ráp ... mǎi |
| credit cards | บัตรเครดิต | bàt krair-dìt |
| travellers cheques | เช็คเดินทาง | chék deun tahng |

# working

| I'm attending a ... | ผม/ดิฉัน | pǒm/dì-chǎn |
| | กำลังรวม ... | gam-lang roo·am ... m/f |
| conference | ที่ประชุม | têe bprà-chum |
| course | ที่อบรม | têe òp-rom |
| meeting | ที่ประชุม | têe bprà-chum |
| trade fair | งานแสดงสินค้า | ngahn sa-daang sǐn káh |

| I'm here for ... | ผม/ดิฉัน | pǒm/dì-chǎn |
| | มาพักที่นี่ ... | mah pák têe née ... m/f |
| (two) days | (สอง) วัน | (sǒrng) wan |
| (three) weeks | (สาม) อาทิตย์ | (sǎhm) ah-tít |

| I'm with ... | ผม/ดิฉัน | pǒm/dì-chǎn |
| | อยู่กับ ... | yòo gàp ... m/f |
| my colleague(s) | เพื่อนงาน | pêu·an ngahn |
| (two) others | อีก (สอง) คน | èek (sǒrng) kon |

**I'm alone.**
อยู่คนเดียว                     yòo kon dee·o

**I have an appointment with ...**
ผม/ดิฉันมีนัดกับ ...          pǒm/dì-chǎn mee nát gàp ... m/f

**I'm staying at the (Bik Hotel), room (10).**
พักอยู่ที่ (โรงแรมบิ๊ก)       pák yòo têe (rohng raam bík)
ที่ห้อง (สิบ)                    hôrng (sìp)

**Where's the (business centre)?**
(ศูนย์ธุรกิจ) อยู่ที่ไหน      (sǒon tú-rá-gìt) yòo têe nǎi

| I need ... | ต้องการ ... | đôrng gahn ... |
| a computer | เครื่อง | krêu·ang |
| | คอมพิวเตอร์ | korm-pew-đeu |
| an internet | ที่ต่อ | têe đòr |
| connection | อินเตอร์เนต | in-đeu-nét |
| an interpreter | ล่าม | lâhm |
| to send a fax | ส่งแฟกซ์ | sòng fàak |

101

| Here's my ... | นี่คือ... ของ | nêe keu ... kŏrng |
| | ผม/ดิฉัน | pŏm/dì-chăn m/f |
| business card | นามบัตร | nahm bàt |
| fax number | เบอร์แฟกซ์ | beu fàak |
| mobile number | เบอร์มือถือ | beu meu těu |
| pager number | เบอร์เครื่องเพจ | beu krêu·ang pét |
| work number | เบอร์ที่ทำงาน | beu têe tam ngahn |

**Can I have your business card?**
ขอมีนามบัตรไหม · kun mee nahm bàt măi

**That went very well.**
ก็ล่วงไปด้วยดีนะ · gôr lôo·ang bai dôo·ay dee ná

**Thank you for your time.**
ขอบคุณที่ให้เวลา · kòrp kun têe hâi wair-lah

**Shall we go for a drink?**
จะไปดื่มกันไหม · jà bai dèum gan măi

**Shall we go for a meal?**
จะไปทานอาหารกันไหม · jà bai tahn ah-hăhn gan măi

**It's on me.**
ผม/ดิฉันเลี้ยงนะ · pŏm/dì-chăn lée·ang ná m/f

# emergencies

| Help! | ช่วยด้วย | chôo·ay dôo·ay |
| Stop! | หยุด | yùt |
| Go away! | ไปให้พ้น | bai hâi pón |
| Thief! | ขโมย | kà-moy |
| Fire! | ไฟไหม้ | fai mâi |

| Call an ambulance! | ตามรถพยาบาล | đahm rót pá-yah-bahn |
| Call a doctor! | เรียกหมอหน่อย | rêe·ak mŏr nòy |
| Call the police! | เรียกตำรวจหน่อย | rêe·ak đam-ròo·at nòy |

**Could you help me, please?**
ช่วยได้ไหม · chôo·ay dâi măi

**I'm lost.**
ผม/ดิฉันหลงทาง · pŏm/dì-chăn lŏng tahng m/f

**Where are the toilets?**
ห้องน้ำอยู่ที่ไหน · hôrng nám yòo têe năi

# Vietnamese

Vietnam — luscious beauty everywhere, from delicate design to technicolour sunsets.

# Pronunciation

| Vowels | | Consonants | |
|--------|---------------|--------|---------------|
| Symbol | English sound | Symbol | English sound |
| a | act | b | bed |
| aa | father | ch | cheat |
| ai | aisle | d | stop |
| aw | saw | đ | dog |
| ay | say | f | fat |
| e | bet | g | go |
| ee | see | ğ | skill |
| er | her | h | hat |
| i | hit | j | joke |
| o | pot | k | kit |
| oh | doh! | l | lot |
| oo | zoo | m | man |
| ow | how | n | not |
| oy | toy | ng | ring |
| u | put | ny | canyon |
| uh | run | p | pet |
| uhr | fur (without 'r') | r | red |
| | | s | sun |
| | | t | top |
| | | v | very |
| | | w | win |
| | | z | zero |

In Vietnamese, vowel sounds can be combined in various ways within a word. In such cases, each vowel should be pronounced separately. In our pronunciation guides we've used dots (eg dee·úhng) to separate the different vowel sounds, but simplified three-vowel combinations to two.

For **tones**, see page 12.

# essentials

| | | |
|---|---|---|
| Yes./No. | *Vâng./Không.* | vuhng/kawm |
| Hello. | *Xin chào.* | sin jòw |
| Goodbye. | *Tạm biệt.* | daạm bee·ụht |
| Please. | *Xin.* | sin |
| Thank you | *Cảm ơn* | ğaảm ern |
| (very much). | *(rất nhiều).* | (zúht nyee·òò) |
| You're welcome. | *Không có gì.* | kawm ğó zeè |
| Excuse me./Sorry. | *Xin lỗi.* | sin lõy |

**Do you speak English?**
*Bạn có nói tiếng Anh không?* baạn ğó nóy dee·úhng aang kawm

**Do you understand?**
*Bạn hiểu không?* baạn heẻ·oo kawm

**I understand.**
*Hiểu.* heẻ·oo

**I don't understand.**
*Không hiểu.* kawm heẻ·oo

# chatting

## introductions

| | | |
|---|---|---|
| Mr | *Ông* | awn |
| Mrs/Miss | *Bà/Cô* | baà/ğaw |

**How are you?**
*Bạn khoẻ không?* baạn kwả kawm

**Fine. And you?**
*Khoẻ. Còn bạn thì sao?* kwả ğòn baạn teè sow

**What's your name?**
*Tên bạn là gì?* den baạn laà zeè

**My name is ...**
*Tên tôi là ...* den doy laà ...

**I'm pleased to meet you.**
*Tôi rất vui được gặp bạn.* doy zúht voo·ee đuhr·ẹrk ğụhp baạn

Vietnamese

105

| | | |
|---|---|---|
| **Here's my ...** | *Đây là ... của tôi.* | đay laà ... ğoò·uh doy |
| **(email) address** | *địa chỉ (email)* | đee·uh jeé (ee·mayl) |
| **phone number** | *số điện thoại* | sáw đee·uhn twại |
| **What's your ...?** | *... của bạn là gì?* | ... ğoò·uh bạan laà zeè |
| **(email) address** | *Địa chỉ (email)* | đee·uh jeé (ee·mayl) |
| **phone number** | *Số điện thoại* | sáw đee·uhn twại |

| | | |
|---|---|---|
| **What's your occupation?** | *Bạn làm nghề gì?* | bạan laàm ngyè zeè |

| | | |
|---|---|---|
| **I'm a ...** | *Tôi là ...* | doy laà ... |
| **businessperson** | *nhà kinh doanh* | nyaà ğing zwaang |
| **student** | *sinh viên* | sing vee·uhn |

| | | |
|---|---|---|
| **Where are you from?** | | |
| *Bạn từ đâu đến?* | | bạan dùhr đoh đén |
| **I'm from (England).** | | |
| *Tôi từ (Anh).* | | doy dùhr (aang) |
| **Are you married?** | | |
| *Bạn lập gia đình chưa?* | | bạan lụhp zaa đìng juhr·uh |

| | | |
|---|---|---|
| **I'm ...** | *Tôi ...* | doy ... |
| **married** | *đã lập gia đình* | đaã lụhp zaa đìng |
| **single** | *độc thân* | đạwp tuhn |

| | | |
|---|---|---|
| **How old are you?** | | |
| *Bạn bao nhiêu tuổi?* | | bạan bow nyee·oo dỏy |
| **I'm ... years old.** | | |
| *Tôi ... tuổi.* | | doy ... dỏy |

## making conversation

| | | |
|---|---|---|
| **What's the weather like?** | | |
| *Thời tiết thế nào?* | | ter·eè dee·úht té nòw |

| | | |
|---|---|---|
| **It's ...** | *Trời ...* | cher·eè ... |
| **cold** | *lạnh* | laạng |
| **(very) hot** | *(rất) nóng* | (zúht) nóm |
| **raining** | *mưa* | muhr·uh |
| **windy** | *gió to* | zó do |

**Do you live here?**
*Bạn sống ở đây không?*     bạạn sáwm èr đạy kawm

**What are you doing?**
*Bạn đang làm gì đấy?*     bạạn đaang laàm zeè đáy

## meeting up

**What time will we meet?**
*Mấy giờ chúng ta sẽ*     máy zèr chúm daa sã
*gặp nhau?*     gụhp nyoh

**Where will we meet?**
*Chúng ta sẽ gặp nhau*     chúm daa sã gụhp nyoh
*ở đâu?*     èr đoh

| | | |
|---|---|---|
| **Let's meet at …** | *Hãy gặp nhau …* | hãy gụhp nyoh … |
| **(eight) o'clock** | *vào lúc (tám) giờ* | vòw lúp (daám) zèr |
| **the entrance** | *tại cửa* | dại gửhr·uh |

**It's been great meeting you.**
*Thật vui được gặp bạn.*     tụht voo·ee đuhr·ẹrk gụhp bạạn

# I love it here!
*Tôi ở đây thích lắm!*
doy ẻr đạy tík lúhm

## likes & dislikes

| | | |
|---|---|---|
| **I thought it was …** | *Tôi nghĩ nó …* | doy ngyeẻ nó … |
| **It's …** | *Nó …* | nó … |
| **awful** | *tồi tệ* | dòy dẹ |
| **great** | *tuyệt vời* | dwee·ụht ver·eè |
| **interesting** | *hay* | hay |
| **Do you like …?** | *Bạn có thích …* | bạạn gó tík … |
| | *không?* | kawm |
| **I (don't) like …** | *Tôi (không) thích …* | doy (kawm) tík … |
| **art** | *nghệ thuật* | ngyẹ twụht |
| **sport** | *chơi thể thao* | jer·ee tẻ tow |

# eating & drinking

**I'd like ..., please.**    *Xin cho tôi ...*    sin jo doy ...

   **the nonsmoking**    *bàn trong khu*    baàn chom koo
   **section**    *không hút thuốc*    kawm hút too·úhk
   **the smoking**    *bàn có hút thuốc*    baàn ğó hút too·úh
   **section**

   **a table for (five)**    *một bàn cho*    mạwt baàn jo
      *(năm) người*    (nuhm) nguhr·eè

**Do you have vegetarian food?**
   *Bạn có đồ chay không?*    bạan ğó đàw jay kawm

**What would you recommend?**
   *Bạn có giới thiệu*    bạan ğó zer·eé tee·oọ
   *những món gì?*    nyũhrng món zeè

## Would you like a drink?
### *Bạn muốn uống gì không?*
bạan moo·úhn oo·úhng zeè kawr

**I'll have ...**    *Cho tôi ...*    jo doy ...
**Cheers!**    *Chúc sức khoẻ!*    júp súhrk kwả

**I'd like (the) ...,**    *Tôi muốn ...*    doy moo·úhn ...
**please.**

   **bill**    *hoá đơn*    hwaá đern
   **drink list**    *thực đơn đồ uống*    tụhrk đern đàw oo
   **menu**    *thực đơn*    tụhrk đern
   **that dish**    *món kia*    món ğee·uh

**(cup of ) coffee/tea**    *(một cốc) càfê/trà*    (mạwt ğáwp) ğaà·fe/ch
**(mineral) water**    *nước (suối)*    nuhr·érk (soo·eé)
**glass of (wine)**    *một cốc (rượu vang)*    mạwt ğáwp (zee·oọ va
**bottle of (beer)**    *một chai (bia)*    mạwt jai (bi·uh)

**breakfast**    *ăn sáng*    uhn saáng
**lunch**    *ăn trưa*    uhn chuhr·uh
**dinner**    *ăn tối*    uhn dóy

**Vietnamese**

# exploring

| Where's the ...? | ... ở đâu? | ... ẽr đoh |
| --- | --- | --- |
| bank | Ngân hàng | nguhn haàng |
| hotel | Khách sạn | kaák saạn |
| post office | Bưu điện | buhr·oo đee·ụhn |

| Where can I find ...? | Tôi có thể tìm các ... ở đâu? | doy ğó tẻ dìm kaák ... ẽr đoh |
| --- | --- | --- |
| clubs | vũ trường | voõ chuhr·èrng |
| pubs | quán rượu | ğwaán zee·oọ |
| restaurants | quán ăn ngon | ğwaán uhn ngon |

**Can you show me (on the map)?**
*Xin chỉ giùm (trên bản đồ này)?*    sin jeẻ zùm (chen baản đàw này)

**What time does it open/close?**
*Mấy giờ nó mở/đóng cửa?*    máy zèr nó mẻr/đáwm ğủhr·uh

**What's the admission charge?**
*Vé vào cửa hết bao nhiêu?*    vá vòw ğủhr·uh hét bow nyee·oo

**When's the next tour?**
*Khi nào là chuyến thăm quan tới?*    kee nòw laà jwee·úhn tuhm ğwaan der·eé

**Where can I buy a ticket?**
*Tôi có thể mua vé ở đâu?*    doy ğó tẻ moo·uh vá ẽr đoh

| One ... ticket to (Saigon), please. | Một vé ... đi (Sài Gòn). | mạwt vá ... đee (saì gòn) |
| --- | --- | --- |
| one-way | một chiều | mạwt jee·oò |
| return | khứ hồi | kúhr hòy |

| My luggage has been ... | Hành lý của tôi đã bị ... | haàng leé ğoỏ·uh doy đaã bẹ ... |
| --- | --- | --- |
| lost | mất | múht |
| stolen | lấy cắp | láy ğủhp |

| Is this the ... to (Huế)? | ... này đi tới (Huế) phải không? | ... này đee der·eé (hwé) faỉ kawm |
| --- | --- | --- |
| bus | Xe buýt | sa bweét |
| plane | Máy bay | máy bay |
| train | Xe lửa | sa lủhr·uh |

Vietnamese

109

| When's the<br>... bus? | *Máy giờ thì chuyến*<br>*xe buýt ... chạy?* | máy zèr tèe chwée·ull<br>sa bwéet ... der·chạy |
|---|---|---|
| first | *đầu tiên* | đòh dee·uhn |
| last | *cuối cùng* | ğoo·eé ğùm |
| next | *kế tiếp* | ğé dee·úhp |
| I'd like a taxi ... | *Tôi muốn một*<br>*chiếc taxi ...* | doy moo·úhn mạwt<br>jee·úhk dúhk·see ... |
| at (9am) | *lúc (chín giờ sáng)* | lúp (jín zèr saáng) |
| tomorrow | *ngày mai* | ngày mai |

**How much is it to ...?**
*Đi đến ... mất bao*     đee đén ... múht bow
*nhiêu tiền?*     nyee·oo dee·ùhn

**Please put the meter on.**
*Xin bật đồng hồ lên.*     sin bụht đàwm hàw len

**Please take me to (this address).**
*Làm ơn đưa tôi tới*     laàm ern đuhr·uh doy der·eé
*(địa chỉ này).*     (dee·ụh jeé này)

**Please stop here.**
*Làm ơn dừng lại ở đây.*     laàm ern zùhrng lại ẻr đay

# shopping

| Where's the (market)? | *(Chợ) ở đâu?* | (jẹr) ẻr đoh |
|---|---|---|
| How much is it? | *Nó bao nhiêu tiền?* | nó bow nyee·oo dee· |
| Can you write<br>down the price? | *Bạn có thể viết giá*<br>*được không?* | bạạn ğó tảy vee·úht z<br>đuhr·ẹrk kawm |
| That's too<br>expensive. | *Cái đó quá đắt.* | ğaí đó ğwaá đúht |
| There's a mistake<br>in the bill. | *Có sự nhầm lẫn trên*<br>*hoá đơn.* | ğó sụhr nyùhm lũhn c<br>hwaá đern |
| It's faulty. | *Nó bị hỏng rồi.* | nó bẹ hóm zòy |
| I'd like ..., please.<br>my change<br>a receipt<br>a refund<br>to return this | *Làm ơn cho tôi ...*<br>*tiền thừa*<br>*hoá đơn*<br>*tiền hoàn lại*<br>*trả lại cái này* | laàm ern jo đay ...<br>dee·ùhn tùhr·uh<br>hwaá đern<br>dee·ùhn hwaàn lạ<br>chaả lại ğaí này |

| Do you accept ...? | Bạn có dùng ... không? | bạạn ğó zùm ... kawm |
| credit cards | thẻ tín dụng | tả dín zụm |
| travellers cheques | séc du lịch | sák zoo lịk |

# working

| I'm attending | Tôi đang tham | doy đaang taam |
| a ... | dự một ... | zụhr mạwt ... |
| conference | hội nghị | họy ngyẹẹ |
| course | hội thảo | họy tỏw |
| meeting | buổi họp | boỏ·ee họp |
| trade fair | hội chợ thương mại | họy jợr tuhr·erng mại |

| I'm with ... | Tôi đến với ... | doy đén ver·eé ... |
| my colleague(s) | đồng nghiệp | dàwm ngyee·ụhp |
| | của tôi | ğoỏ·uh doy |
| (two) others | (hai) người khác | (hai) nguhr·eè kaák |

**I'm here for (two) days/weeks.**
Tôi ở đây (hai) ngày/tuần.   doy ẻr đay (hai) ngày/dwùhn

**I'm alone.**
Tôi đến một mình.   doy đén mạwt mìng

**I have an appointment with ...**
Tôi có hẹn với ...   doy ğó hạn ver·eé ...

**I'm staying at the (Hoa Binh Hotel), room (21).**
Tôi ở khách sạn (Hoà Bình)   doy ẻr kaák sạạn (hwaà bìng)
phòng (hai mươi mốt).   fòm (hai muhr·ee mạwt)

| Where's the ...? | ... ở đâu? | ... ẻr đoh |
| conference | Hội nghị | họy ngyẹẹ |
| meeting | Buổi họp | boỏ·ee họp |

| I need ... | Tôi cần ... | doy ğùhn ... |
| a computer | một máy tính | mạwt máy díng |
| an internet | vào mạng | vòw maạng |
| connection | | |
| an interpreter | một người | mạwt nguhr·eè |
| | phiên dịch | fee·uhn zịk |
| to send a fax | gửi một | gúhr·ee mạwt |
| | bản fax | baản faak |

*Vietnamese*

| | | |
|---|---|---|
| **Here's my ...** | *Đây là ... của tôi.* | đay laà ... ğoỏ·uh doy |
| business card | *danh thiếp* | zaang tee·úhp |
| fax number | *số fax* | sáw faak |
| mobile number | *số điện thoại* | sáw đee·ụhn twaị |
| | *di động* | zee đạwm |

**Can I have your business card?**
*Xin bạn cho tôi danh thiếp*  sin baạn jo doy zaang tee·úhp
*của bạn.*  ğoỏ·uh baạn

**That went very well.**
*Buổi họp có kết quả tốt rồi.*  boỏ·ee họp ğó ğét ğwaả dáwt zòy

**Shall we go for a drink?**
*Mời bạn đi uống nước.*  mer·eè baạn đee oo·úhng nuhr·é

**Shall we go for a meal?**
*Mời bạn đi ăn cơm.*  mer·eè baạn đee uhn ğerm

**It's on me.**
*Tôi mời bạn.*  doy mer·eè baạn

# emergencies

| | | |
|---|---|---|
| **Help!** | *Cứu tôi với!* | ğuhr·oó doy vér·ee |
| **Stop!** | *Dừng lại đi!* | zùhrng laị dee |
| **Go away!** | *Đi đi!* | đee đee |
| **Thief!** | *Cướp!* | ğuhr·érp |
| **Fire!** | *Cháy!* | jáy |

**Call an ambulance!**
*Gọi một xe cứu thương!*  gọy mạwt sa ğuhr·oó tuhr·erng

**Call a doctor!**
*Gọi bác sĩ!*  gọy baák seẽ

**Call the police!**
*Gọi cảnh sát!*  gọy ğaảng saát

**Could you help me, please?**
*Làm ơn giúp đỡ?*  laàm ern zúp đẽr

**I'm lost.**
*Tôi bị lạc.*  doy beẹ laạk

**Where are the toilets?**
*Nhà vệ sinh ở đâu?*  nyaà vẹ sing ér đoh

# 24 hours
# in the city

Enjoying a city break? Hit the streets and savour every second . . .

# Bangkok

**9am** Start your day with top egg-noodle soup with wontons and red pork. Ferry your way down the river, checking out the city's monuments in a breezy, nonpolluted kind of way.

**1pm** Treat yourself to soft-shelled crab with glass noodles at In Love restaurant at Thewet Pier, a fine riverside lunch stop, then skytrain to Siam from Saphan Taksin for the requisite shopping.

**3.30pm** Leave time for a calming swim, a Thai massage and a tasty bag of mangosteens to wrap up your afternoon.

**6pm** Enjoy classy sunset drinks at Vertigo in the Banyan Tree Hotel. For local street food in the warping heat, try the car park on the corner of Ratchadamri Road and Soi Sarasin.

**9pm** Drink to your Bangkok success with G&Ts at Cheap Charlie's on Sukhumvit Soi 11, followed by great live music at Admaker's.

**12am** Don't forget the midnight snack and the walk through the human zoo of Khao San Road – it's the perfect time to watch messier-than-you bar hordes spill onto the street.

24 hours in the city

114

# Beijing

**6am** Worship the dawn in the Temple of Heaven Park and take in the beauty of the early-morning t'ai chi practitioners.

**8am** Act like a local and get around the *hútòng* lanes on a bike. Check out the Qing dynasty courtyards as you go. Celebrate with a breakfast of dumplings and Yanjing beer.

**11am** Explore the Forbidden City's astonishing imperial apartments and temples. Go under the Gate of Heavenly Peace, shop for communist memorabilia in the underpass and gaze up at the kite-flying once you hit Tiananmen Square.

**3pm** Have a late lunch of Beijing duck with plum sauce on your way to Liulichang Street, perfect for antique browsing.

**5pm** Watch the sunset from the Summer Palace, then enjoy some snacks and drinks on Lotus Lane. Top it off with a jaunt to the Peking Opera.

**12am** Not to be missed — a midnight boat ride on magical Houhai Lake.

# Hanoi

**6am** Enjoy the city's (almost) silent morning. Wander to Hoan Kiem Lake and its ghostly grey-blue mist, watching the crumbling stucco buildings of the Old Quarter greet the day.

**10am** Fortify yourself with a *pho* (noodle soup) breakfast and a fluffy fresh baguette, and pay your respects to Uncle Ho, now residing in the Ho Chi Minh Mausoleum.

**12pm** Take a break by reading a good book in the quiet of the Temple of Literature, then satisfy your hunger and your conscience at KOTO restaurant (all proceeds go towards helping street children).

**3pm** Spend your afternoon shopping at Pho Nha Tho. Afterwards, watch the shadows of St Joseph's Cathedral grow longer.

**7pm** Dine on squid with dill at Bia Hoi Viet, a *bia hoi* (beer tavern), on Pho Tong Dan, then catch a Vietnamese pop star at the Hanoi Opera House. Wrap it up with a motorbike ride around West Lake.

**10.45pm** Get to Highway 4 for rice wine on the roof before 11pm and while the night away from on high.

24 hours in the city

# Hong Kong

**6am** Walk through Hong Kong Park and be entranced by the t'ai chi faithful and the birds in the Edward Youde Aviary. Treat yourself to a hearty egg-something breakfast at Eating Plus in the IFC Mall.

**8.30am** Step outside, squint up at the city's tallest building (Two IFC), then jam yourself into the Star Ferry to head to Kowloon, on the other side of Victoria Harbour.

**11am** Check out the view of the Island from Tsim Sha Tsui's promenade, and nibble some street snacks as you walk up the Golden Mile. Breathe in the commercial chaos and pay your respects to the authentically decrepit Chungking Mansions.

**3pm** Observe the stallholders setting up for the Temple Street Night Market, then head south on the MTR for dim sum at Hoi Yat Heen.

**6pm** Rock your way back across on the ferry and catch the Peak Train for the fantastic late afternoon views from Victoria's Peak.

**8pm** Head to the Mid-Levels and watch Hong Kong life through the bar windows before embracing the night in Lan Kwai Fong.

# Jakarta

**8am** Start at the Pasar Ikan (fish market) near the old Dutch port of Sunda Kelapa. Check out the hive of morning activity, and afterwards the Museum Bahari cataloguing the history of the Dutch East India Company.

**11am** Take a 'kiddie seat' on a bike to Taman Fatahillah (the old town square) and check out the Jakarta History Museum and Dutch-designed surrounds of the Kota area. Keep on soaking up the vibe with a well-earned coffee break at Cafe Batavia.

**3pm** Pass through Lapangan Merdeka (Freedom Square) and see Soekarno's National Monument, then take yourself to Taman Mini Indonesia Indah – the whole of Indonesia in just one park.

**5pm** Get yourself some arts and crafts at Jakarta's flea market, or head to Plaza Senayan for designer souvenirs for your friends.

**8pm** Dine on nasi goreng at Jasa Bundo, then sample a cultural show at Taman Ismail Marzuki. Dance the night away at Bugils (from the Indonesian for 'Crazy Westerner' – you'll fit in just fine).

24 hours in the city

# Phnom Penh

**7.30am** Go for an early morning stroll north along the banks of the Mekong River. Watch the fishermen work their nets, then settle in for a coffee-and-croissant breakfast in one of the riverfront cafés.

**10am** Browse the Psar Kandal market and haggle for a tasty mango or rambutan. On a more serious note, head to the Tuol Sleng Museum (a testament to the crimes of the Khmer Rouge) for a better understanding of where Cambodia is today.

**1pm** Let the somewhat faded Art Deco masterpiece of the Psar Thmei draw you in for lunch among the steamy soup stalls. Browse the Popil Photo Gallery, part of Phnom Penh's growing art scene.

**4pm** Hire a river boat and relax on a two-hour cruise along the Tonlé Sap and up the Mekong River.

**6.30pm** Happy-hour cocktails at the Elephant Bar of Hotel Le Royal are a classic, followed by dinner at Frizz restaurant.

**9pm** Wind down with drinks at the Foreign Correspondent Club or Rubies, and don't forget to people-watch.

# Seoul

**8am** The day begins with a spicy cold-noodle breakfast among the stainless steel counters in Namdaemun market, complemented with a surround-sound encounter with Korea's eating customs.

**10am** Check out the brave new world of Seoul's A-list, the shopping and entertainment district of Apgujeong that's part commercial centre and part shrine to the Korean beauty cult.

**12pm** Eat barbecue to your stomach's content at Samwon Garden, then burn off the protein with a walk around Seoul Tower.

**3pm** Roam the Gyeongbokgung palace to soak up the atmosphere of the feudal royal court and move on to Hurest Spa for some bathhouse-induced euphoria.

**6pm** Join the hustle of workers and students on Myeong Dong's streets and try out the green tea-plus-desserts in the teashops.

**8pm** head to one of many tiny underground venues around Hongkik University, Seoul's live indie music hotspot, and boogie the night away.

# Tokyo

**6am** Get up early to watch frozen fish being flung about at Tsukiji Market. Sample a fresh sushi breakfast before you move on to Meiji-jing, Tokyo's most elegant Shinto shrine, surrounded by serene forest and an impressive *torii* (temple gate).

**10am** Get yourself on a train bound for Shimo-Kitazawa, a maze of little alleys alive with tiny secondhand stores, artsy indie designers and cool cafés. Lunch on cold soba noodles and pick up some funky delights.

**1pm** Tone down your afternoon with a trip to Senso-ji, a living temple where the smells of incense and rice crackers mingle.

**4pm** Soak and scrub your cares away at Jakotsu-yu, at the Edo-era *onsen* (traditional bathhouse).

**6pm** Savour your dinner with *yakitori* (grilled skewers of chicken or vegetables) at the ever-busy Akiyoshi.

**8pm** Watch sumo at the Ryogoku Kukugikan Stadium, though you'd have to be a *yakuza* (Japanese Mafia) to get a good seat.

# Vientiane

**9am** Get into the Vientiane vibe early with a trip to the labyrinthine morning market. Head out of town to spend the morning checking out Buddhist and Hindu sculptures at Xieng Khuan (Buddha Park).

**1pm** Get back in time to lunch on a *bo bûn* (a cold Vietnamese noodle dish) at PVO, then drop into the commercial district around Th Lan Xang to eye off the haughty Lao Arc de Triomphe, Patuxai.

**3pm** Your afternoon should be spent at the beautiful Pha That Luang, the monument to Buddhist religion and Lao sovereignty. Check out the stupa and the cloisters, and don't miss the light of the setting sun on the golden roof. Top it off with a Beer Lao by the Mekong at dusk at Sunset Sala Khounta.

**7pm** Dine at the Ban Anou night market in Vientiane's Chinatown, then sample some local life with a Lao Traditional Show in Th Manthaturath. For a slick evening of daiquiris, try Deja Vu's equally slick white interior.

24 hours in the city

# Yangon

**6am** You guessed it – the crack of dawn is the best time to meditate with the t'ai chi artists at Mahabandoola Garden. Afterwards, head to the sprawling Bogyoke Aung San Market for lacquerware and fabrics.

**10am** Before lunch, spend a moment's reflection in a prayer hall at Shwedagon Paya, a glittering gold-leaf-covered stupa said to house eight hairs of the Buddha.

**12pm** Lunch on *lethouq* (a spicy salad of raw vegetables dressed with lime juice, onions, peanuts and chillies) and roll a cheroot at a street-side stall. If you're really tough, try smoking a 2cm-thick one.

**3pm** Take a rickshaw around town for the mobile sightseeing tour and hop out when you spot a *chinlon* (cane ball) game ... and the players' gravity-defying pirouettes. Get in shape for the next match at a Burmese kick-boxing class at Yangon University.

**6pm** Wind down with a cup of syrupy tea and *mohinga* (a fish-based noodle soup) in the balmy afternoon at one of Yangon's famous teashops, and hang out with the locals to end your day.

Index

125

ternal photographs from iStockphoto (except for p115): p114 Floating market,
ngkok – Kate Shephard • p115 Bike riders passing the entrance to the Forbidden
y, Beijing – Andrew J Loiterton/Getty Images • p116 Street vendor, Hanoi – Jakob
tner • p117 Night scene, Hong Kong – Billy Chan • p118 National Monument,
:arta – Hasimsyah Samosir • p119 Huge temple, Phnom Penh – Ron Sumners •
.20 Imperial palace (Gyeongbokgung), Seoul – Andy Hwang • p121 Taxi in the sky-
:aper district, Tokyo – Juergen Sack • p122 Tuk-tuk, Vientiane – Anthony Brown •
23 Young Buddhist monks at Shwedagon Pagoda, Yangon – Christine Gonsalves

# What kind of traveller are you?

**A.** You're eating chicken for dinner *again* because it's the only word you know.

**B.** When no one understands what you say, you step closer and shout louder.

**C.** When the barman doesn't understand your order, you point frantically at the beer.

**D.** You're surrounded by locals, swapping jokes, email addresses and experiences – other travellers want to borrow your phrasebook or audio guide.

## If you answered A, B, or C, you NEED Lonely Planet's language products ...

- **Lonely Planet Phrasebooks** – for every phrase you need in every language you want

- **Lonely Planet Language & Culture** – get behind the scenes of English as it's spoken around the world – learn and laugh

- **Lonely Planet Fast Talk & Fast Talk Audio** – essential phrases for short trips and weekends away – read, listen and talk like a local

- **Lonely Planet Small Talk** – 10 essential languages for city breaks

- **Lonely Planet Real Talk** – downloadable language audio guides from lonelyplanet.com to your MP3 player

## ... and this is why

- **Talk to everyone everywhere**
  Over 120 languages, more than any other publisher

- **The right words at the right time**
  Quick-reference colour sections, two-way dictionary, easy pronunciation, every possible subject – and audio to support it

# Lonely Planet Offices

| **Australia** | **USA** | **UK** |
|---|---|---|
| 90 Maribyrnong St, Footscray, | 150 Linden St, Oakland, | 2nd floor, 186 City Rd, |
| Victoria 3011 | CA 94607 | London EC1V 2NT |
| ☎ 03 8379 8000 | ☎ 510 893 8555 | ☎ 020 7106 2100 |
| fax 03 8379 8111 | fax 510 893 8572 | fax 020 7106 2101 |
| ✉ talk2us@lonelyplanet.com.au | ✉ info@lonelyplanet.com | ✉ go@lonelyplanet.co.uk |

## lonelyplanet.com